# ROMANTICISM

Romantic writers worked during one of the most momentous epochs of western cultural history. It was an epoch defined by responses to the revolutionary politics which were epitomized by the French Revolution. *Romanticism* traces the major writers, terms and debates associated with the genre. It surveys various readings by contemporaries of Romanticism and brings the survey up to date by considering post-structuralist, new-historicist and gender-oriented perspectives on the subject. Overall, the book argues that the politically radical aspects of literature of the period would more usefully be described as 'late Enlightenment', while the term Romantic may be taken to define, among other things, an essentially conservative tendency of thought.

Aidan Day summarizes changing views of Romanticism in relation to what has, until recently, been seen as the canon of British Romantic writers: William Blake, William Wordsworth, Samuel Taylor Coleridge, Lord Byron, Percy Bysshe Shelley and John Keats. The writings of these poets, still the basis of many readings of Romanticism, are placed in the context of political and philosophical thinkers such as Edmund Burke, Thomas Paine and Mary Wollstonecraft. At the same time, the issues raised in the book are discussed in relation to a wide range of other writers of the period, both canonical and non-canonical, from Jane Austen and Robert Burns to Charlotte Smith and Anna Laetitia Barbauld.

*Romanticism* is an accessible, succinct and up-to-date introductory textbook. It is tailor-made for students new to the subject, who will find it essential reading and a solid base for further study.

**Aidan Day** is Reader in English Literature at the University of Edinburgh. He is co-editor, with Christopher Ricks, of *The Tennyson Archive*, a 31-volume reproduction of Tennyson's poetical manuscripts in facsimile. He is the editor of *Alfred Lord Tennyson: Selected Poems* and *Robert Browning: Selected Poetry and Prose*. He is also the author of *Jokerman: Reading the Lyrics of Bob Dylan*.

# THE NEW CRITICAL IDIOM

SERIES EDITOR: JOHN DRAKAKIS, UNIVERSITY OF STIRLING

*The New Critical Idiom* is an invaluable series of introductory guides to today's critical terminology. Each book:

- provides a handy, explanatory guide to the use (and abuse) of the term
- offers an original and distinctive overview by a leading literary and cultural critic
- relates the term to the larger field of cultural representation.

With a strong emphasis on clarity, lively debate and the widest possible breadth of examples, *The New Critical Idiom* is an indispensable approach to key topics in literary studies.

- See below for new books in this series.

*Gothic* by Fred Botting
*Historicism* by Paul Hamilton
*Ideology* by David Hawkes
*Metre, Rhythm and Verse* by Philip Hobsbaum
*Romanticism* by Aidan Day

# ROMANTICISM

Aidan Day

LONDON AND NEW YORK

First published 1996
by Routledge
11 New Fetter Lane, London EC4P 4EE

Simultaneously published in the USA and Canada
by Routledge
29 West 35th Street, New York, NY 10001

© 1996 Aidan Day

Typeset by Keystroke, Jacaranda Lodge, Wolverhampton

Printed and bound in Great Britain by Clays Ltd, St Ives PLC

*British Library Cataloguing in Publication Data*
A catalogue record for this book is available from the British Library

*Library of Congress Cataloging in Publication Data*
Day, Aidan.
    Romanticism / Aidan Day.
        p.   cm. — (The New Critical Idiom Series)
    Includes bibliographical references (p.).
    1. English literature —19th century — History and criticism —
    Theory, etc.   2. English literature — 18th century — History and
    criticism —Theory, etc.   3. Romanticism — Great Britain.   I. Title.
    II. Series.
    PR457.D38   1996
    820.9'145—dc20        95-8288

ISBN 0–415–12266–X (hbk)
ISBN 0–415–08378–8 (pbk)

Til Charlotte og Asta

# CONTENTS

# SERIES EDITOR'S PREFACE

*The New Critical Idiom* is a series of introductory books which seeks to extend the lexicon of literary terms, in order to address the radical changes which have taken place in the study of literature during the last decades of the twentieth century. The aim is to provide clear, well-illustrated accounts of the full range of terminology currently in use, and to evolve histories of its changing usage.

The current state of the discipline of literary studies is one in which there is considerable debate concerning basic questions of terminology. This involves, among other things, the boundaries which distinguish the literary from the non-literary; the position of literature within the larger sphere of culture; the relationship between literatures of different cultures; and questions concerning the relation of literary to other cultural forms within the context of interdisciplinary studies.

It is clear that the field of literary criticism and theory is a dynamic and heterogenous one. The present need is for individual volumes on terms which combine clarity of exposition with an adventurousness of perspective and a breadth of application. Each volume will contain as part of its apparatus some indication of the direction in which the definition of particular terms is likely to move, as well as expanding the disciplinary boundaries within which some of these terms have been traditionally contained. This will involve some re-situation of terms within the larger field of cultural representation, and will introduce examples from the area of film and the modern media in addition to examples from a variety of literary texts.

# PREFACE

Romanticism was a European phenomenon. But while this book is given the general title *Romanticism*, it is designed as an introductory survey for students of literature in English, and its primary subject is British Romanticism. There are surveys of the various continental European Romantic movements in, for example, *Romanticism in National Context*, edited by Roy Porter and Mikuláš Teich (Cambridge, 1988).

What has for many years been seen as the canon of British Romantic writers – centring on the poets Blake, Wordsworth, Coleridge, Byron, Shelley and Keats – still forms the basis of many curricula in the teaching of British Romanticism. These poets are, then, the writers I have referred to most commonly in this book. I have surveyed the ways in which the nature of that canon has been conceived and reconceived, particularly during the latter half of the twentieth century. At the same time, the canon has itself been brought into question by recent historicist and feminist critics. Such critics have emphasized the need not merely to reconsider the magic six male poets but to attend anew to the large number of other authors in the period. Some of these authors – Jane Austen is an example – are canonical in literary terms, though not 'Romantic', and have received plenty of critical attention. But many are simply not canonical in any terms. I have on occasion referred to such non-canonical authors. But for fuller selections from these writers, I would refer readers to Duncan Wu's *Romanticism. An Anthology* (Blackwell, 1994) and to Jerome McGann's *The New Oxford Book of Romantic Period Verse* (Oxford University Press, 1994).

Finally, throughout this book, where I have quoted, I have tended to quote extensively. This is a principle to which I have adhered partly because it gives the flavour of the writers I mention, both primary and secondary, better than a summary, and partly because there are times when the writers simply put better what they have to say than I could.

# Acknowledgements

My thanks go to Karina Williamson and John Drakakis for the advice they gave me during the writing of this book.

# INTRODUCTION

Let me begin with some quotations. The first is from the fifth edition of *The Oxford Companion to English Literature*, where Romanticism is described as

> a literary movement, and profound shift in sensibility, which took place in Britain and throughout Europe roughly between 1770 and 1848. Intellectually it marked a violent reaction to the Enlightenment. Politically it was inspired by the revolutions in America and France . . . . Emotionally it expressed an extreme assertion of the self and the value of individual experience . . . together with the sense of the infinite and the transcendental. Socially it championed progressive causes . . . . The stylistic keynote of Romanticism is intensity, and its watchword is 'Imagination'.

(Drabble 1985: 842–43)

The second quotation is from the sixth edition of M.H. Abrams' *A Glossary of Literary Terms*. Here, under the heading 'Neoclassic and Romantic', Abrams tells us first of all that, as he applies them, the 'Neoclassic' and 'Romantic' periods in Britain are 'names for periods of literature'. The '"Neoclassic Period" in England spans the 140 years or so after the Restoration (1660), and the "Romantic Period" is usually taken to extend approximately from the outbreak of the French Revolution in 1789 – or alternatively, from the publication of [Wordsworth and Coleridge's] *Lyrical Ballads* in 1798 – through the first three decades of the nineteenth century' (Abrams 1993: 125). Abrams goes on to summarize his sense of the ways in which Romantic ideals and writings differ most conspicuously from those of the Neoclassic period. The summary is worth quoting at length:

(1) The prevailing attitude favored innovation as against traditionalism in the materials, forms, and style of literature. Wordsworth's Preface to the second edition of *Lyrical Ballads* in 1800 was written as a poetic 'manifesto', or statement of revolutionary aims, in which he denounced the poetic diction of the preceding century and proposed to deal with materials from 'common life' in 'a selection of language really used by men'. Wordsworth's serious or tragic treatment of lowly subjects in common language violated the basic neoclassic rule of decorum, which asserted that the serious genres should deal only with high subjects in an appropriately elevated style. Other innovations in the period were the exploitation by Samuel Taylor Coleridge [1772–1834], John Keats [1795–1821], and others of the realm of the supernatural and of 'the far away and the long ago'; the assumption by William Blake [1757–1827], William Wordsworth [1770–1850], and Percy Bysshe Shelley [1792–1822] of the persona of a poet–prophet who writes a visionary mode of poetry; and the use of poetic symbolism (especially by Blake and Shelley) deriving from a world-view in which objects are charged with a significance beyond their physical qualities.

(2) In his Preface to *Lyrical Ballads* Wordsworth repeatedly declared that good poetry is 'the spontaneous overflow of powerful feelings'. According to this point of view poetry is not

primarily a mirror of men in action; on the contrary, its essential element is the poet's own feelings, while the process of composition, since it is 'spontaneous', is the opposite of the artful manipulation of means to foreseen ends stressed by the neoclassic critics . . . . The philosophical-minded Coleridge substituted for neoclassic 'rules', which he describes as imposed by the poet from without, the concept of the inherent organic 'laws' of the poet's imagination; that is, he conceives that each poetic work, like a growing plant, evolves according to its internal principles into its final organic form.

(3) To a remarkable degree external nature – the landscape, together with its flora and fauna – became a persistent subject of poetry, and was described with an accuracy and sensuous nuance unprecedented in earlier writers. It is a mistake, however, to describe the romantic poets as simply 'nature poets'. While many major poems by Wordsworth and Coleridge – and to a great extent by Shelley and Keats – set out from or return to an aspect or change of aspect in the landscape, the outer scene is not presented for its own sake but only as a stimulus for the poet to engage in the most characteristic human activity, that of thinking.

(4) Neoclassic poetry was about other people, but much of romantic poetry invited the reader to identify the protagonists with the poets themselves, either directly, as in Wordsworth's *Prelude* (1805; revised 1850) and a number of romantic Lyric poems . . . or in altered but recognizable form, as in Lord Byron's [1788–1824] *Childe Harold* (1812–18).

(5) What seemed the infinite social promise of the French Revolution in the early 1790s, fostered the sense in writers of the early Romantic Period that theirs was a great age of new beginnings and high possibilities. Many writers viewed a

human being as endowed with limitless aspiration toward the infinite good envisioned by the faculty of imagination.

(Abrams 1993: 127–29)

There is a good deal of congruence, despite the differences in length, between the accounts of Romanticism given in the *Oxford Companion* and in the *Glossary*. The dates vary somewhat, but both sources agree on a centre of gravity for Romanticism at the end of the eighteenth century and the beginning of the nineteenth. They both agree that Romanticism was in some sense at odds with Neoclassic or Enlightenment attitudes and values (an entry on 'Enlightenment' in the *Glossary* uses the term to define 'an intellectual movement and cultural ambience' which runs roughly parallel with the 'Neoclassic Period' in literature; Abrams 1993: 52). Both accounts agree on the inspirational role of the French Revolution in Romantic ideology and on a democratic or progressively rebellious impulse at the heart of that ideology. Both agree that Romanticism gave a special importance to individual experience, that the faculty of imagination was of special significance and that this faculty was celebrated along with a profound sense of spiritual reality.

Agreement with a number or, indeed, all of these points is frequently found in twentieth-century commentary on Romanticism. To take a few examples at random: Derek Roper notes that the 'beginning of the Romantic movement in English poetry is usually dated from the first publication of *Lyrical Ballads* in 1798' (Roper 1987: 8); Sir Maurice Bowra has observed that if 'we wish to distinguish a single characteristic which differentiates the English Romantics from the poets of the eighteenth century, it is to be found in the importance which they attached to the imagination and in the special view which they took of it' (Bowra 1950: 1); Harold Bloom and Lionel Trilling can be found saying that 'the virtual identity between High Romanticism and Revolution marks the French visionary, Jean-Jacques Rousseau [1712–78], as the central man of Romantic tradition' (Bloom and Trilling 1973: 5). In a celebrated essay, 'The Concept of "Romanticism" in Literary History', René Wellek throws the net wider:

> If we examine the characteristics of the actual literature which called itself or was called 'romantic' all over the continent, we find throughout Europe the same conceptions of poetry and of the workings and nature of poetic imagination, the same conception of nature and its relation to man, and basically the same poetic style.
>
> Turning to England, we can see a complete agreement with the French and Germans on all essential points. The great poets of the English romantic movement constitute a fairly coherent group, with the same view of poetry and the same conception of imagination, the same view of nature and mind. They share also a poetic style, a use of imagery, symbolism, and myth, which is quite distinct from anything that had been practised by the eighteenth century, and which was felt by their contemporaries to be obscure and almost unintelligible.
>
> (Wellek 1949: 147, 158–59)

The problem is that any such attempts to summarize Romanticism inevitably end up over-systematising and simplifying the phenomenon. They imply a coherence (Wellek indeed speaks explicitly of coherence) which closer inspection leads us to call in question. It is true that some of the elements by which Romanticism is defined in the summaries do appear in the writings of those who are now called Romantic. But it is not true that all British Romantic writers display all of those elements all of the time. The summaries which tend to unify Romanticism avoid, in the first place, recognition of the fact that any of the writers who are labelled Romantic may have changed or, at least, shifted opinion in the course of a writing career. Secondly, some of the defining features of Romanticism in the summaries do not, as they are described in outline, fit easily together. We hear that

Romanticism was a reaction against Enlightenment perspectives and Neoclassical aesthetics and at the same time that it was inspired by the French Revolution. But the French Revolution was in part a direct expression of the French Enlightenment. *L'Encyclopédie* (1751–72) was one of the great monuments of the French Enlightenment and helped to lay the intellectual foundations of the Revolution. As the *Encyclopaedia Britannica* tells us: *L'Encyclopédie* 'takes for granted the justice of religious tolerance and speculative freedom. It asserts in distinct tones the democratic doctrine that it is the common people in a nation whose lot ought to be the main concern of the nation's government' (*Encyclopaedia Britannica* 1910–11: VIII. 204).

Rather, then, than providing an overview of something called Romanticism and fitting individual writers into that overview, I shall begin this book by taking some of the topics which recur in the summaries and attempting to trace the position of individual writers in relation to those topics. Later in the book it will be possible to reflect on the questions of whether there is anything coherent about Romanticism in general and, if there can indeed be said to have been any sort of coherence, whether this conforms to the widely established stereotypes. I shall start with Wordsworth and Coleridge's *Lyrical Ballads* which has so often been taken, as the *Oxford Companion* reminds us, as 'a landmark of English Romanticism and the beginning of a new age' (Drabble 1985: 596). The relationship between this collection of poems and the age it is often seen as having displaced, the age of Neoclassicism and Enlightenment, needs to be established.

# 1

## ENLIGHTENMENT OR ROMANTIC?

In 1954 Robert Mayo published an important article in which he compared the poems published by Wordsworth and Coleridge as *Lyrical Ballads* with poems published in contemporary magazines and miscellanies. What Mayo discovered was that far from marking 'the beginning of a new age' the poems of *Lyrical Ballads* were in many respects the flowering of an already established age. By 'age', here, I do not mean to define the entirety of a culture. The taste and values which inform the *Lyrical Ballads* were not the sole, or even the prevailing, taste and values of later eighteenth-century British culture. But they were the taste and values of a significant part of that culture. And this part, as Mayo observes, expressed itself in periodical publications that were themselves a part of the cultural mainstream:

> We have been asked to consider too exclusively the revolutionary aspects of the *Lyrical Ballads* . . . . there is a conventional side to the *Lyrical Ballads*, although it is usually overlooked. . . . they . . . conformed in numerous ways to the modes of

1798, and reflected popular tastes and attitudes. . . . There is in much of the magazine verse of the 1790s a literary lag of at least half a century. In his attacks on Pope, Gray, Prior, and Dr Johnson in the 1802 Appendix [to the third edition of *Lyrical Ballads*] Wordsworth was not exactly beating dead horses. . . . The insipidity of magazine poetry, however, is deceptive. It is not uniformly antique, and it is far from being homogeneous. A persistent minority . . . are occupied with new subjects of poetry and written in the new modes of the late eighteenth century. . . . With the poems of this minority the *Lyrical Ballads* have a great deal in common. . . . In general, the drift is in several directions only – towards 'nature' and 'simplicity', and towards humanitarianism and sentimental morality. . . . the reader of that day would tend to construe most of the contents of the *Lyrical Ballads* in terms of these modes of popular poetry, with which he was already familiar.

(Mayo 1954: 486, 488–90)

In the pages that follow I am going to look in more detail at the two tendencies in which Mayo sees the *Lyrical Ballads* immersed: first, humanitarian sentiment and second, an emphasis on nature.

## HUMANITARIANISM

The drift towards humanitarianism noted by Mayo in 1790s poetry is evident in several poems from *Lyrical Ballads*. There is, for instance, Wordsworth's 'The Female Vagrant'. A version of this poem had formed part of a longer work, 'Salisbury Plain', which was initially composed, though not published, in 1793–94. The speaker of 'The Female Vagrant', the vagrant herself, recounts how her father, a poor cottager, was driven out of his property at the hands of a wealthy and acquisitive neighbour:

Then rose a mansion proud our woods among,
And cottage after cottage owned its sway,
No joy to see a neighbouring house, or stray

Through pastures not his own, the master took;
My Father dared his greedy wish gainsay;
He loved his old hereditary nook,
And ill could I the thought of such sad parting brook.

But, when he had refused the proffered gold,
To cruel injuries he became a prey,
Sore traversed in whate'er he bought and sold.
His troubles grew upon him day by day,
Till all his substance fell into decay.
His little range of water was denied;
All but the bed where his old body lay,
All, all was seized, and weeping, side by side,
We sought a home where we uninjured might abide.

(39–54; Brett and Jones 1976: 45–46)

The woman and her father found such a home through the man that the woman married. But this was no more than a temporary respite. After the death of her father a few years later an 'evil time' (91; Brett and Jones 1976:47) returned and the woman and her three new children followed her husband who, of necessity, had to go to fight for the British during the American War of Independence (1775–81). Wordsworth's disgust at such war emerges in the woman's statements in the fourteenth stanza:

Oh! dreadful price of being to resign
All that is dear *in* being! better far
In Want's most lonely cave till death to pine,
Unseen, unheard, unwatched by any star;
Or in the streets and walks where proud men are,
Better our dying bodies to obtrude,
Than dog-like, wading at the heels of war,
Protract a curst existence, with the brood
That lap (their very nourishment!) their brother's blood.

(118–26; Brett and Jones 1976: 48–49)

The woman lost her husband and children 'by sword/And ravenous plague' (132–33; Brett and Jones 1976:49). She managed to return to England and was cast upon the life of destitute wandering that we find her living at the opening of 'The Female Vagrant'. As she says in the penultimate stanza of the poem:

> I lived upon the mercy of the fields,
> And oft of cruelty the sky accused;
> On hazard, or what general bounty yields,
> Now coldly given, now utterly refused.
> The fields I for my bed have often used.
>
> (253–57; Brett and Jones 1976: 53–54)

R.L. Brett and A.R. Jones comment that as 'The Female Vagrant' stands in 1798 'it is clearly a product of the revolutionary Wordsworth, whose passionate humanitarianism leads him to write about the injustices of a social system which oppresses the poor and turns them into outcasts' (Brett and Jones 1976: 280–81).

Alongside Wordsworth's anger at social injustice in 'The Female Vagrant' may be placed Coleridge's complaint, in 'The Dungeon', at the social forces – poverty and lack of education – which generate criminal behaviour and at the dehumanizing prison conditions which convicted criminals are made to suffer:

> And this place our forefathers made for man!
> This is the process of our love and wisdom,
> To each poor brother who offends against us –
> Most innocent, perhaps – and what if guilty?
> Is this the only cure? Merciful God?
> Each pore and natural outlet shrivell'd up
> By ignorance and parching poverty,
> His energies roll back upon his heart,
> And stagnate and corrupt; till changed to poison,
> They break out on him, like a loathsome plague-spot;

Then we call in our pamper'd mountebanks –
And this is their best cure! Uncomforted
And friendless solitude, groaning and tears,
And savage faces, at the clanking hour,
Seen through the steams and vapour of his dungeon,
By the lamp's dismal twilight! So he lies
Circled with evil, till his very soul
Unmoulds its essence, hopelessly deformed
By sights of ever more deformity!

(1–19; Brett and Jones 1976: 82)

Wordsworth and Coleridge's humanitarian protests were poetically highly refined and often specially subtle. But there was nothing particularly original in the humanitarian topics themselves. Robert Mayo points out that

However much they may be rendered fresh and new by poetic treatment, it must be recognized that most of the objects of sympathy in [Lyrical Ballads] belong to an order of beings familiar to every reader of magazine poetry – namely, bereaved mothers and deserted females, mad women and distracted creatures, beggars, convicts and prisoners, and old people of the depressed classes, particularly peasants. For nearly every character, portrait, or figure, there is some seasoned counterpart in contemporary poetry. . . . Wordsworth's Female Vagrant. . . . is one of a familiar class of outcasts, the female beggar; and through that class she is associated with the long procession of mendicants who infested the poetry departments of the Lady's Magazine, the Edinburgh Magazine, and other popular miscellanies in the last years of the eighteenth century. Some of the mendicant poems are merely portraits, which make blunt appeals to sympathy for the poor, the aged, and the unhappy (as does Wordsworth's Old Man Travelling – more subtly); but others are narrative poems, sometimes, like The Female Vagrant, told in the first person and emphasizing the

> contrast between past joy and present sorrow, the horrors of
> war and its consequences, man's treatment of man, and the
> indifference of society.
>
> (Mayo 1954: 495, 500–501)

The fashionableness of humanitarian sympathy was part of the ground-swell of radical political feeling in the last quarter of the eighteenth century, the period which saw first the American War of Independence and then the French Revolution.

The success of the American colonies in achieving independence was seen by many as a vindication of basic human rights and it was celebrated by groups in Britain who were campaigning for reform in the system of Parliamentary representation, a system which had a restrictive base in the aristocracy and land-owning class. The reform movement drew heavily on the Nonconformist and Dissenting population of the country which suffered under legally inscribed civil and religious disabilities: the Corporation Act of 1661 and the Test Act of 1673 together proscribed dissenters from holding government office and from entering the Universities of Oxford and Cambridge. The reformist groups, stirred by the American example, gained further stimulation from the French Revolution and the first half of the 1790s was a momentous period for the radical cause in Britain. But while it was certainly encouraged by events in France, that cause was also to a large extent home-grown. Its shape in the 1790s was directed by the writings of a native Englishman who had spent the mid-1770s to the later 1780s in America. In 1776 Thomas Paine (1737–1809) published, in America, a pamphlet entitled *Common Sense*, which argued for equality of rights amongst American citizens, for American independence and for the establishment of republican government on American soil. Paine's most influential work in Britain, *Rights of Man*, was published in two parts, the first in 1791 and the second in 1792. Paine's dissenting background (his father was a Quaker staymaker from Norfolk) and his reformist zeal bear witness to the way in which a native tradition of radical thought flowered in the light of the French Revolution. As E.P. Thompson has written in *The Making of the English Working Class*:

> Too often events in England in the 1790s are seen only as a reflected glow from the storming of the Bastille. But the elements precipitated by the French example – the Dissenting and libertarian traditions – reach far back into English history. And the agitation of the 1790s, although it lasted only five years (1792–6) was extraordinarily intensive and far-reaching. . . . It was an English agitation, of impressive dimensions, for an English democracy.
>
> Constitutionalism was the flood-gate which the French example broke down. But the year was 1792, not 1789, and the waters which flowed through were those of Tom Paine.
>
> (Thompson 1991: 111)

Paine's *Rights of Man* was written as a reply to Edmund Burke's *Reflections on the Revolution in France*, a work first published in 1790 and which stands as the classic conservative denunciation of the French Revolution. Burke (1729–97) was a Whig politician who reacted against widespread Whig support, in the early years after 1789, for the revolutionary French. The immediate occasion which prompted Burke to write the *Reflections* was his reading of a sermon applauding the French Revolution delivered to the Revolution Society in late 1789 by the Unitarian radical Dr Richard Price (1723–91). The Revolution Society had been established in 1788 to mark the centenary of the English 'revolution' of 1688, when Parliament had declared in favour of the Protestant William of Orange as King over and against the Catholic James II. That declaration signalled a crucial transfer of power in the state from the monarchy to Parliament and one hundred years later many Englishmen initially saw in the French Revolution a repetition of what had happened fairly peacefully in England the previous century. Burke was much more suspicious of the happenings in France and argued that the drive for equality across the Channel would involve a drive towards violence and tyranny rather than peace and liberty. He identified French revolutionary change with a fanatical attachment to theory, that contravened the accumulated experience and wisdom of centuries of slow political change. His rhetoric is charged with the conservative's dread of anarchy should the existing, long-established institutions of the land be challenged:

> What is that cause of liberty, and what are those exertions in its favour, to which the example of France is so singularly auspicious? Is our monarchy to be annihilated, with all the laws, all the tribunals, and all the antient corporations of the Kingdom? Is every land-mark of the country to be done away with in favour of a geometrical and arithmetical constitution? Is the house of lords to be voted useless? Is episcopacy to be abolished? Are the church lands to be sold to Jews and jobbers; or given to bribe new-invented municipal republics into a participation in sacrilege? . . . Are all orders, ranks, and distinctions to be confounded, that out of universal anarchy, joined to national bankruptcy, three or four thousand democracies should be formed into eighty-three, and that they may all, by some sort of unknown attractive power, be organized into one?
>
> (Burke 1986: 144)

The actual course of events in revolutionary France would, as the years went on, seem to bear out many of Burke's worst fears and his book became a mainstay for the reactionary ascendancy that took root in Britain from the middle of the 1790s onwards. But his passionate antagonism towards the Revolution in France was understood by many in the earlier 1790s as an iniquitous defence of the vested interests of the Establishment in Britain, a defence which simply failed to engage or even to comprehend the issues of human rights raised by the French Revolution. This was the line that Tom Paine took in his defence of the Revolution in *Rights of Man*.

Where Burke had argued for the authority of precedent and tradition, Paine saw in the invocation of precedent only a means of repression in the present:

> Government by precedent, without any regard to the principle of the precedent, is one of the vilest systems that can be set up. In numerous instances, the precedent ought to operate as a warning, and not as an example, and requires to be shunned instead of imitated; but instead of this, precedents are taken in the lump, and put at once for constitution and for law.
>
> Either the doctrine of precedents is policy to keep a man in a state of ignorance, or it is a practical confession that wisdom degenerates in governments as governments increase in age, and can only hobble along by the stilts and crutches of precedents.
>
> (Paine 1985: 196)

Paine's attack on the principle of precedent went hand in hand with an attack on the principle of hereditary rule by monarchy and aristocracy and with a eulogy of genuinely representative government:

> All hereditary government is in its nature tyranny. An heritable crown, or an heritable throne ... have no other significant explanation than that mankind are heritable property. To inherit a government, is to inherit the people, as if they were flocks and herds. . . .
>
> I smile to myself when I contemplate the ridiculous insignificance into which literature and all the sciences would sink, were they made hereditary; and I carry the same idea into governments. An hereditary governor is as inconsistent as an hereditary author. . . .
>
> ... in whatever manner the separate parts of a constitution may be arranged, there is *one* general principle that distinguishes freedom from slavery, which is, that all *hereditary*

> *government over a people is to them a species of slavery, and*
> *representative government is freedom.*
>
> (Paine 1985: 172, 176, 201)

E.P. Thompson observes that Paine 'destroyed with one book century-old taboos' and that the fifth chapter, especially, of the second part of *Rights of Man* 'set a course towards the social legislation of the twentieth century' (Thompson 1991: 100, 102). In this chapter Paine proposed

> a graduated income tax ... paying out the moneys raised
> or saved in sums to alleviate the position of the poor. He
> proposed family allowances: public funds to enable general
> education of all children: old age pensions ... a maternity
> benefit, a benefit for newly-wedded couples ... and the build-
> ing in London of combined lodging-houses and workshops to
> assist immigrants and unemployed.
>
> (Thompson 1991: 102)

What Paine established, Thompson writes, 'was a new rhetoric of radical egalitarianism' (Thompson 1991: 103). His book sold in very large numbers and Paine 'dominated the popular radicalism of the early 1790s' (Thompson 1991: 108).

This radicalism was manifest in the large number of societies – based in London and in northern British cities such as Manchester and Glasgow – which were committed to the cause of achieving reform in Parliamentary suffrage. Some of these societies had roots going back far into the eighteenth century, such as the London Society for Constitutional Information, whose leading lights in the early 1790s were men such as the philologist John Horne Tooke (1736–1812) and the dramatist Thomas Holcroft (1745–1809); others, like the somewhat more artisan London Corresponding Society, which was led by the shoemaker Thomas Hardy, and the radical lecturer and poet John Thelwall (1764–1834), were estab-lished after the Revolution in France had intensified radical feeling in the country. Along with the activities of societies such as these went the enterprise of a bookseller and publisher, Joseph Johnson (1738–1809). Johnson's circle of radical middle-class writers and artists, all of whom he supported and encouraged and several of whom he published, included Paine himself; the political theoretician and novelist William Godwin (1756–1836); the feminist intellectual Mary Wollstonecraft (1759–97); William Wordsworth; William Blake; the Swiss artist and friend of William Blake, Henry Fuseli (1741–1825); and the leading Unitarian and radical intellectual, Joseph Priestley (1733–1804). Johnson's circle was dominated by religious dissenters like Priestley, but the dissenting community, which imparted such a large amount of energy to the radical movement as a whole, was itself not a homogeneous or unified body of people. E.P. Thompson has written of the bewildering variety of dissenting sects and splinter groups which characterized much of the radical or Jacobin movement in Britain. He has also identified in the weirder fringes of the London dissenting population a context for the productions of William Blake:

> No easy summary can be offered as to the Dissenting tradition which was one of the elements precipitated in the English Jacobin agitation. It is its diversity which defies generalization. . . . Here are Unitarians or Independents, with a small but influential artisan following. . . . There are the Sandemanians . . . the Moravians with their communitarian heritage; the Inghamites, the Muggletonians, the Swedenborgian sect which originated in a hairdresser's off Cold Bath Fields and which published a *Magazine of Heaven and Hell*. . . . There are the Calvinist Methodist immigrants from Wales, and immigrants brought up in the Covenanting sects of Scotland. . . . And there are curious societies, like the Ancient Deists of Hoxton, who spoke of dreams and (like Blake) of conversations with departed souls and Angels, and who (like Blake) 'almost immediately yielded

to the stronger impulse of the French Revolution' and became *'politicians'*.

... Against the background of London Dissent, with its fringe of deists and earnest mystics, William Blake seems no longer the cranky untutored genius that he must seem to those who know only the genteel culture of the time. On the contrary, he is the original yet authentic voice of a long popular tradition.

(Thompson 1991: 55–56)

William Blake had begun one of his best known works, *Songs of Innocence*, in 1784–85, though the collection was not issued until 1789–90. Amongst the songs is one, 'The Little Black Boy', which stresses the equality of souls between black boy and white English boy. The poem is written 'in the spirit of contemporary radical anti-slavery writing' (Stevenson and Erdman 1971: 58) and turns on the conceit that the black boy has the spiritual generosity to imagine aiding the soul of the white boy to bear the presence of God, when they both have lost the masks of black or white skin. It might be argued that Blake's focus on spiritual states in this poem deflects attention away from the practical and mundane contingencies of slavery. It could also be argued that the assertion of spiritual excellence in the black child may be seen as offering a ground for action in the real world:

My mother bore me in the southern wild,
And I am black . . .
White as an angel is the English child . . .

My mother taught me underneath a tree . . .

Look on the rising sun: there God does live
And gives his light, and gives his heat away . . .

And we are put on earth a little space,
That we may learn to bear the beams of love,

And these black bodies and this sun-burnt face
Is but a cloud, and like a shady grove.

For when our souls have learn'd the heat to bear
The cloud will vanish we shall hear his voice . . .

thus I say to little English boy.
When I from black and he from white cloud free,
And round the tent of God like lambs we joy:

Ill shade him from the heat till he can bear,
To lean in joy upon our father's knee.

(1–3, 5, 9–10, 13–18, 22–26; Erdman and Bloom 1970: 9)

This poem, as W.H. Stevenson and David Erdman observe, situates Blake with those writers of the 1780s – including poets such as William Cowper (1731–1800) or Ann Yearsley (1756–1806) – who aligned themselves with that branch of enlightened, humanitarian feeling that sought the abolition of slavery. The first anti-slavery society in Britain was formed by Quakers in 1783 and in 1786 Thomas Clarkson (1760–1846) published an *Essay on the Slavery and Commerce of the Human Species*. The publication of this anti-slavery *Essay* brought Clarkson into touch with William Wilberforce (1759–1833) and, with the foundation in 1787 of a committee for the abolition of the slave trade, there began the long agitation which finally led to the abolition of the British slave trade in 1807. As opposition to slavery continued after the 1780s, so it formed part of the broad humanitarian movement that was spurred by the French Revolution and the 1790s were marked by a rash of anti-slavery poems. In 1791, for example, Anna Laetitia Barbauld (1743–1825) composed her 'Epistle to William Wilberforce' in order to mark the rejection by Parliament of a bill proposed by Wilberforce for preventing the further importation of slaves to British colonies:

> Cease, Wilberforce, to urge thy generous aim!
> Thy Country knows the sin, and stands the shame!
> The Preacher, Poet, Senator in vain
> Has rattled in her sight the Negro's chain . . .
> >             Still Afric bleeds,
> Unchecked, the human traffic still proceeds;
> She stamps her infamy to future time,
> And on her hardened forehead seals the crime.
> >             (1–4, 15–18; Barbauld 1825: I. 173–74)

In 1794 Robert Southey (1774–1843) produced a series of sonnets protesting at the institution of slavery:

> High in the air exposed the Slave is hung,
> > To all the birds of Heaven, their living food!
> He groans not, though awaked by that fierce Sun
> > New tortures live to drink their parent blood!
> He groans not, though the gorging Vulture tear
> > The quivering fibre! Hither gaze, O ye
> Who tore this Man from Peace and Liberty!
> >             (Sonnet VI, 1–7; Southey 1823: I. 38)

Again, in 1799, Thomas Campbell complained against slavery in *The Pleasures of Hope*. 'Was man ordain'd the slave of man to toil,/Yok'd with the brutes, and fetter'd to the soil . . . ?' (I. 495–96; Campbell 1799: 38). Campbell indulges in a stereotypical, primitivist vision of an African chief as 'noble savage' in order to make his point:

> Lo! once in triumph, on his boundless plain,
> The quiver'd chief of Congo lov'd to reign;
> With fires proportion'd to his native sky,
> Strength in his arm, and light'ning in his eye . . .
> > The plunderer came: – alas! no glory smiles
> For Congo's chief on yonder Indian isles;
> Forever fallen! no son of Nature now,

> With Freedom charter'd on his manly brow!
> Faint, bleeding, bound, he weeps the night away.
>
> (l. 503–506, 510–15; Campbell 1799: 39)

Anti-slavery sentiment became common in the magazine poetry to which Robert Mayo refers in order to establish the contemporaneity of the humanitarian ideas of Wordsworth and Coleridge's *Lyrical Ballads*, even though Wordsworth and Coleridge themselves did not take up this particular issue in their volume (Mayo 1954: 495).

In the years following the French Revolution William Blake's poetic expression of his radical sympathies grew even more pronounced. In *America* (1793–94) he retrospectively celebrated the American Revolution as a triumph of life and liberty over the death-dealing oppression of British rule. At the opening of the 'Prophecy' section of the poem the governing power of Britain ('The Guardian Prince of Albion') threatens a group of American leaders, including Thomas Paine, with ominous fire and blood:

> The Guardian Prince of Albion burns in his nightly tent,
> Sullen fires across the Atlantic glow to America's shore:
> Piercing the souls of warlike men, who rise in silent night,
> Washington, Franklin, Paine & Warren, Gates,
>   Hancock & Green;
> Meet on the coast glowing with blood from Albions
>   fiery Prince.
>
> Washington spoke; Friends of America look over the
>   Atlantic sea;
> A bended bow is lifted in heaven, & a heavy iron chain
> Descends link by link from Albion's cliffs across the sea
>   to bind
> Brothers & sons of America.
>
> (3. 1–9; Erdman and Bloom 1970: 51)

The success of the Americans in throwing off the binding chain is acclaimed in its own right in this poem. But the War of Independence is also taken as a type of what Blake envisaged as a universal energy of revolution which would sweep away all tyrannies. The spirit of this revolutionary energy is characterized as Orc who, early in *America*, uses a biblical language of resurrection and renewal as he imagines the dawn of a new world of freedom:

> The morning comes, the night decays, the watchmen leave their
>     stations;
> The grave is burst, the spices shed, the linen wrapped up;
> The bones of death, the cov'ring clay, the sinews shrunk
>     & dry'd.
> Reviving shake, inspiring move, breathing! awakening!
> Spring like redeemed captives when their bonds & bars
>     are burst;
> Let the slave grinding at the mill, run out into the field:
> Let him look up into the heavens & laugh in the bright air;
> Let the inchained soul shut up in darkness and in sighing,
> Whose face has never seen a smile in thirty weary years;
> Rise and look out, his chains are loose, his dungeon doors
>     are open.
> And let his wife and children return from the opressors
>     scourge;
> They look behind at every step & believe it is a dream.
> Singing. The Sun has left his blackness, & has found a fresher
>     morning
> And the fair Moon rejoices in the clear & cloudless night;
> For Empire is no more, and now the Lion & Wolf shall cease.
>
> (6. 1–15; Erdman and Bloom 1970: 52)

This kind of apocalyptic rhetoric is typical of the large hopes encouraged in some British minds in the first place by the American Revolution but most importantly by the French Revolution.

The hope of freedom from literal empire was only one aspect of Blake's radical thought. He desired at the same time freedom from what he saw as the restricting and repressive moral codes and institutions of contemporary society – not least the institution of marriage. Blake may be understood as having seen contemporary society as a hierarchically oppressive system that, in its denial of civil rights, particularly to married women, succeeded in trapping women within an institution that was a practical and mental prison. Blake knew the feminist thinker Mary Wollstonecraft from the radical London circle – centred around the bookseller Joseph Johnson – in which they both moved during the early 1790s. In 1792 Johnson published Wollstonecraft's *A Vindication of the Rights of Woman*, a work which claimed the same human rights for women as were being claimed by others for men. The social position of women (especially, though by no means exclusively, married women) was severely disadvantaged in the later eighteenth century. Miriam Brody has commented on 'the "civil death" of women' that was

> written into the *Commentaries on the English Constitution* (1758) by William Blackstone, the distinguished and learned professor of law at Oxford. 'By marriage', interprets Blackstone,
>> the husband and wife are one person in law; that is, the very being or legal existence of the woman is suspended during the marriage or at least is incorporated and consolidated into that of the husband; under whose wing, protection and cover, she performs everything.
>
> A married woman, then, could legally hold no property in her own right, nor enter into any legal contract, nor for that matter claim any rights over her own children. . . . the woman's dependence on the economic productivity of her husband . . . achieved a legal sanctity in Blackstone which formed the spirit, as well as the letter, of all traditional injunctions to women which writers on the subject would make.
>
> (Wollstonecraft 1992: 30–31)

In *A Vindication* Wollstonecraft herself quotes from one such writer on the subject, Dr James Fordyce, who published addresses to women concerning their nature and conduct in 1765 and 1776. Wollstonecraft offers his account of the situation of married women as an exemplum of contemporary attitudes and she employs the familiar liberal language concerning slavery and tyranny to classify the situation so described:

> Is not the following portrait – the portrait of a house slave? 'I am astonished at the folly of many women, who are still reproaching their husbands for leaving them alone ... for treating them with this and the other mark of disregard or in-difference; when, to speak the truth, they have themselves in a great measure to blame. ... had you behaved to them with more *respectful observance*, and a more *equal tenderness; studying their humours, overlooking their mistakes, submitting to their opinions* in matters indifferent, passing by little instances of unevenness, caprice or passion, giving *soft* answers to hasty words, complaining as seldom as possible ... had you pursued this conduct, I doubt not but you would have maintained and even increased their esteem ... and your house might at this day have been the abode of domestic bliss.' Such a woman ought to be an angel – or she is an ass – for I discern not a trace of the human character, neither reason nor passion in this domestic drudge, whose being is absorbed in that of a tyrant's.
>
> (Wollstonecraft 1992: 198)

A comparable point to Wollstonecraft's was put in 1795 by Maria Edgeworth (1767–1849) in her *Letters for Literary Ladies*. In the fourth of her letters between Julia and Caroline, Edgeworth has Caroline write concerning Julia's 'intended separation from her husband' (Edgeworth 1805: 148). In the closing lines of the following passage Caroline comments with bitter irony on the control over women that contemporary society granted to married men:

From domestic uneasiness a man has a thousand resources.
. . . If his home become tiresome, he leaves it; if his wife become
disagreeable to him, he leaves her, and in leaving her loses *only*
a wife. But what resources has a woman? – Precluded from all
the occupations common to the other sex, she loses even those
peculiar to her own. She has no remedy, from the company of a
man she dislikes, but a separation; and this remedy, desperate
as it is, is allowed only to a certain class of women in society;
to those whose fortune affords them the means of subsistence.
. . . A peeress then probably can leave her husband if she wish
it; a peasant's wife cannot; she depends upon the character and
privileges of a wife for actual subsistence. Her domestic care,
if not her affection, is secured to her husband; and it is just
that it should. He sacrifices his liberty, his labour, his ingenuity,
his time, for the support and protection of his wife; and in
proportion to his protection, is his power.

(Edgeworth 1805: 153–54)

Mary Wollstonecraft's view of the slavery of women may directly
have influenced Blake in his composition of *Visions of the
Daughters of Albion* (1793). In this poem Blake draws parallels
between shackled black slaves and the way in which the human
kind of his own country are caught within imprisoning institu-
tional codes, within entrapping modes of perception and customs.
Blake has one of his speakers, a female named Oothoon, attack first
the custom of tithing (where the church could claim a percentage
of farmers' earnings) before she moves into a wider attack on
the oppressions of a theocratic state that incarcerates women in
marriage. Blake sees such incarceration as engendering an
appalling perversion of the spirit:

With what sense does the parson claim the labour of
    the farmer?
What are his nets & gins & traps. & how does he surround
    him

With cold floods of abstraction, and with forests of solitude,
To build him castles and high spires. where kings & priests
  may dwell.
Till she who burns with youth. and knows no fixed lot; is bound
In spells of law to one she loaths: and must she drag the chain
Of life, in weary lust! must chilling murderous thoughts. obscure
The clear heaven of her eternal spring?

           (5. 17–24; Erdman and Bloom 1970: 47–48)

Blake's assaults on spiritual, economic and political repression
and his celebration of the revolutionary instances of America and
France found parallels in the 1790s in the work of British writers
such as Helen Maria Williams (1762–1827), Robert Burns
(1759–96) and Charlotte Smith (1748–1806). In her *Letters from
France*, published in 1792, Helen Maria Williams – to whom
Wordsworth had addressed his first published poem in 1787,
'Sonnet on Seeing Miss Helen Maria Williams Weep at a Tale of
Distress' – eulogized the Revolution in France in a poem entitled
'To Dr Moore, in Answer to a Poetical Epistle Written by Him in
Wales'. Here she exults in the freedoms gained by the poor as a
result of the Revolution:

Delightful land! ah, now with general voice
Thy village sons and daughters may rejoice;
Thy happy peasant, now no more – a slave . . .
Oppression's cruel hand shall dare no more
To seize with iron grip his scanty store,
And from his famished infants wring those spoils,
The hard-earned produce of his useful toils;
For now on Gallia's plains the peasant knows
Those equal rights impartial heaven bestows.

           (27–29, 33–38; Lonsdale 1990: 417)

Williams continues in this poem to condemn thinkers (such as
Edmund Burke) who seek to preserve an essentially mediaeval state

organization. She contrasts feudalism with what had happened in France, where the darkness of such an organization of the state had been banished by the light of reason:

> Auspicious Liberty! in vain thy foes
> Deride thy ardour, and thy force oppose;
> In vain refuse to mark thy spreading light . . .
> Those reasoners who pretend that each abuse,
> Sanctioned by precedent, has some blest use! . . .
> Must feudal governments for ever last,
> Those Gothic piles, the work of ages past?
> Nor may obtrusive reason boldly scan,
> Far less reform, the rude, mishapen plan?
> The winding labyrinths, the hostile towers . . .
> The lonely dungeon in the caverned ground;
> The sullen dome above those central caves,
> Where lives one despot and a host of slaves? –
> Ah, Freedom, on this renovated shore
> That fabric frights the moral world no more!
>
> (43–45, 49–50, 53–57, 60–64; Lonsdale 1990: 417)

In her earlier *Letters Written in France*, first published in 1790, Williams displays an unbridled enthusiasm for what she describes as 'an event so sublime as the French revolution' (Williams 1792: 65). In the ninth of these letters she writes:

> Whether the new constitution be composed of durable materials or not, I leave to politicians to determine; but it requires no extra-ordinary sagacity to pronounce, that the French will henceforth be free. The love of liberty has pervaded all ranks of the people, who, if its blessings must be purchased with blood, will not shrink from paying the price:
>
> > 'While ev'n the peasant boasts his rights to scan,
> > And learns to venerate himself as man.'
>
> The enthusiastic spirit of liberty displays itself, not merely on

the days of solemn ceremonies ... but is mingled with the gaiety of social enjoyment. When they converse, liberty is the theme of discourse.

(Williams 1792: 70)

''Tis Liberty's bold note I swell' declared Robert Burns in the first verse of his 1794 'Ode for General Washington's Birthday', where he pays homage to the leader of the American revolutionaries. In the second verse of this poem Burns moves into both a condemnation of worthless people who accept despotism and an acclamation of those who, like the liberty-seeking Americans under Washington, exemplify the highest nature of human beings:

> Where is Man's godlike form?
> Where is that brow erect and bold,
> That eye that can, unmoved, behold
> The wildest rage, the loudest storm,
> That e'er created fury dared to raise!
> Avaunt! thou caitiff, servile, base,
> That tremblest at a Despot's nod,
> Yet, crouching under th'iron rod,
> Canst laud the arm that struck th'insulting blow!
> Art thou of man's imperial line?
> Each sculking feature answers, No!
> But come, ye sons of Liberty,
> Columbia's offspring, brave as free,
> In danger's hour still flaming in the van:
> Ye know, and dare maintain, the Royalty of Man.

(13–28; Kinsley 1968: II. 732–33)

Burns' commitment to the ideal of freedom – political freedom and its concomitant, the freedom to read and write freely – was apparent in his earlier 'Here's a Health to them that's awa', published in 1792:

> May Liberty meet wi' success!
> May Prudence protect her frae [from] evil!
> May Tyrants and Tyranny tine [get lost] i' the mist
> And wander their way to the devil!
>
> . . .
>
> Here's freedom to him that wad [would] read,
> Here's freedom to him that wad write!
> There's nane [none] ever fear'd that the Truth should be heard,
> But they whom the Truth wad indite.
>
> (13–16, 21–24; Kinsley 1968: II. 663)

Burns' ironic appropriation, in the second verse of the Washington Ode, of terms like 'imperial line' and 'Royalty' to describe the character of people who are not what is conventionally meant by 'imperial' and 'royal', but who are ordinary people whose lives are founded in freedom and democracy, is paralleled again in the sentiment of one of his best known songs: 'For a' that and a' that', published in 1795. This poem, again written in a mixture of Scots and English, occupies, as James Kinsley has noted, a 'central place in the psalmody of radicalism' (Kinsley 1968: III. 1467). Burns here shows his contempt for empty distinctions of rank and his conviction of a common brotherhood of 'Man':

> Is there, for honest Poverty
>     That hings [hangs] his head, and a' [all] that;
> The coward-slave, we pass him by,
>     We dare be poor for a' that!
>   For a' that, and a' that,
>     Our toils obscure, and a' that,
>   The rank is but the guinea's stamp,
>     The Man's the gowd [gold] for a' that. –
>
> What though on hamely [plain] fare we dine,
>     Wear hoddin grey [coarse cloth], and a' that.

> Gie [give] fools their silks, and knaves their wine,
>   A Man's a Man for a' that.
>
> . . .
>
> Then let us pray that come it may,
>   As come it will for a' that,
> That Sense and Worth, o'er a' the earth
>   Shall bear the gree [come off best], and a' that.
>   For a' that, and a' that,
>     Its comin yet for a' that,
>   That Man to Man the warld [world] o'er,
>     Shall brothers be for a' that. –
>
> (1–12, 33–40; Kinsley 1968: II. 762–63)

The yearning that 'Sense and Worth' should come off best 'o'er a' the earth' was the principal impulse behind the writing of Charlotte Smith's 1793 novel *The Old Manor House*. The hero of this work, Orlando Somerive, is the younger son of an impoverished branch of a well-to-do family. He falls in love with Monimia, the orphaned and poor relative of Mrs Lennard, housekeeper to the aristocratic Mrs Rayland. Mrs Rayland, who lives at Rayland Hall, is the last surviving and very rich member of another branch of the same family as Orlando. The difference in class between Monimia and Orlando means that they have to keep their affair secret, partly in order that Orlando should not incur the displeasure of Mrs Rayland and thereby fail to be named her heir. In order to gain some kind of income Orlando has to take a commission in the army. This draws him away from Monimia and to North America where he has to fight for the British against the American rebels. After a fairly complicated series of events during his campaign in America, Orlando returns to England. Here he discovers that Mrs Rayland has died, that Rayland Hall is deserted, that Monimia has disappeared, and that he has been cheated out of his inheritance by the stewards of Mrs Rayland's estate. After much to-ing and fro-ing and numerous happy accidents, Orlando recovers the Rayland estate, marries Monimia and everyone, including Orlando's mother and sisters, lives happily ever after.

At one level *The Old Manor House* reads like genteel romantic fiction, as indeed, up to a point, it is. Charlotte Smith herself was without money and, having left her emotionally and financially unreliable husband in 1788, had to support a large family by her writing. Her characterization and plot-structure are certainly designed to be palatable – and hence saleable – to the respectable middle-class audience upon whom she depended. This said, however, there are many elements in *The Old Manor House* which bespeak Charlotte Smith's radical leanings. On his voyage to America, for example, we hear Orlando beginning to question the legitimacy of the war he is employed to fight:

> He frequently took the night watch. . . . On these occasions sleep would not always befriend him; and then all that he had left, his Monimia, his family, the Hall, the rural happiness he had enjoyed in his native country, forcibly presented themselves in contrast to the wretchedness around him; and when he considered a number of men thus packed together in a little vessel, perishing by disease; such of them as survived going to another hemisphere to avenge on a branch of their own nation a quarrel, of the justice of which they knew little, and were never suffered to enquire, he felt disposed to wonder at the folly of mankind, and to enquire again *what all this was for?*
>
> (Smith 1987: 336)

Orlando's growing unease about the war shades off into the author's explicit disgust at the base, self-serving motives of those in government who had voted to pursue this effectively internecine conflict:

> the modern directors of war . . . incurred no personal danger, nor gave themselves any other trouble than to raise money

from one part of their subjects, in order to enable them to destroy another. . . . The provisions on board were universally bad. . . . But it was all for *glory*. And that the ministry should, in thus purchasing glory, put a little more than was requisite into the pockets of contractors, and destroy as many men by sickness as by the sword, made but little difference in an object so infinitely important; especially when it was known (which, however, Orlando did not know) that messieurs the contractors were for the most part members of parliament, who under other names enjoyed the profits of a war, which, disregarding the voices of the people in general, or even of their own constituents, they voted for pursuing. Merciful God! can it be thy will that mankind should thus tear each other to pieces. . . . Can it be thy dispensation that kings are entrusted with power only to deform thy works.

(Smith 1987: 337–38)

Charlotte Smith pursues this criticism of the nature of British power throughout her novel. Mrs Rayland, 'the only survivor of the three co-heiresses of Sir Hildebrand Rayland' (Smith 1987: 3), with all her scorn for those without titles and money, is seen as the survivor of an antiquated and vicious social system. Smith sees education and the exercise of reason as the prime means of redeeming this society, as when Orlando encourages Monimia to understand the idea of equality of rights:

Her poverty, her dependence, the necessity of her earning a subsistence by daily labour, had been the only lessons she had been taught. . . .

But she had learned now that, abject and poor as she was, she was an object of affection to Orlando. . . . The reading he had directed her to pursue, had assisted in teaching her some degree of self-value. She found that to be poor was not disgraceful in the eye of Heaven, or in the eyes of the good upon earth.

(Smith 1987: 47)

Janet Todd has observed of *The Old Manor House*:

> Although she presented only the American struggle for rights, Charlotte Smith insisted on making parallels with the French Revolution, while, even more provocatively, she ensured that no reader could finish her novel without concluding that there were many elements in British society that richly deserved a revolution as well.
>
> (Smith 1987: x)

But this radical message was carefully embedded within a conventional narrative that could simultaneously satisfy conservative and complacent expectations.

Wordsworth and Coleridge themselves were involved in the upsurge of radical feeling in the early 1790s. Wordsworth, who had visited Charlotte Smith in Brighton in 1791 (Gill 1989: 51), wrote one of his most radical documents in the year that *The Old Manor House* was published. In early 1793 Richard Watson, Bishop of Llandaff, published an Appendix to accompany a Sermon which he had preached in 1785. In his Appendix Watson expressed indignation at the news of the beheading of the French King Louis XVI on 21 January 1793. Watson had been in favour of the French Revolution at its outbreak, but now he was alienated and he argued in his Appendix against those British radicals who, in his opinion, having failed to recognize the time-honoured excellencies of the present British constitution, would repeat the ills of France in their search for liberty, equality and fraternity. In *A Letter to the Bishop of Llandaff* Wordsworth replied to Richard Watson's Appendix, though the *Letter* was not published in Wordsworth's lifetime. The *Letter* is written, as Wordsworth declares, in 'a republican spirit' (Owen and Smyser 1974: I. 31) and it appears to have been influenced, at least in part, by Paine's *Rights of Man*. Wordsworth starts out by defending the execution of Louis XVI as a necessary evil (Owen and Smyser 1974: I. 33–34) before going on to condemn aristocratic and monarchical rule:

> Reflecting on the corruption of the public manners, does your lordship shudder at the prostitution which miserably deluges our streets? You may find the cause in our aristocratical prejudices. . . . Do you lament that such large portions of mankind should stoop to occupations unworthy the dignity of their nature? You may find in the pride and luxury thought necessary to nobility how such servile arts are encouraged. . . . If the long equestrian train of equipage should make your lordship sigh for the poor who are pining in hunger, you will find that little is thought of snatching the bread from their mouths to eke out the 'necessary splendor' of nobility.
>
> I have not time to pursue this subject farther, but am so strongly impressed with the baleful influence of aristocracy and nobility upon human happiness and virtue that if, as I am persuaded, monarchy cannot exist without such supporters, I think that reason sufficient for the preference I have given to the republican system.
>
> (Owen and Smyser 1974: I. 45–46)

A comparable indignation at the injustices of contemporary British society – at poverty and at exploitative warmongering – informs Wordsworth's poem *Salisbury Plain*, which he composed from the summer of 1793 to the spring of 1794. *Salisbury Plain* contains what was to become 'The Female Vagrant' and opens with stanzas that suggest that life for the 'hungry savage', where at least all other savages are 'naked and unhouzed', is preferable to a world where it is possible for the underprivileged to reflect 'on the state/Of those who on the couch of Affluence rest' (3, 1, 23–24; Gill 1975: 21). The poem proceeds to tell the story of a homeless man, '[b]y thirst and hunger pressed' (42; Gill 1975: 22), who is crossing Salisbury Plain and who meets someone similarly hard-pressed, the female vagrant. In 1795 Wordsworth began elaborating the narrative of *Salisbury Plain* when he turned it into *Adventures on Salisbury Plain*. In *Adventures* the homeless man is a sailor and an outlaw. He had undertaken some war service,

returned home and been press-ganged into another tour of duty.
When this second long tour – 'For years the work of carnage did
not cease' (82; Gill 1975: 125) – was over, the sailor 'urged his
claim' (91; Gill 1975: 125) for a financial gratuity. This was
refused and he returned to Britain destitute. Desperate to provide
something for his family, this essentially good man robbed and
murdered a traveller whom he had met when very nearly home.
He never succeeded in returning to his wife. Now on the run on
Salisbury Plain, the sailor meets the female vagrant, hears her story
of how she lost her husband and children in war, and a little later
comes across another woman, '[a] single woman, lying spent and
gone' (698; Gill 1975: 150). It turns out that this second woman
is his wife, turned out of her parish by those who suspected that it
was her husband who had murdered the traveller. The sailor, guilty
of murder and of ruining his family, begs his wife for forgiveness.
She dies and he hands himself in to the law. The poem ends with
his body dangling on a gibbet. One of the special interests of
*Adventures on Salisbury Plain* is that it shows something of the
influence of another of the radical theoretical works of the early
1790s, William Godwin's *Enquiry Concerning Political Justice*
(1793). As Nicholas Roe has commented:

> Wordsworth's sailor is a benevolent man betrayed into crime
> and then punished by the society he has served: he is dis-
> charged with no quittance, murders to provide for his family,
> and is finally executed by 'the slaves of Office' whose negligence
> forced him to commit the crime in the first place. An immediate
> influence upon 'the vices of the penal law' as represented in the
> sailor's story was Godwin's necessarian argument that criminal
> behaviour was the product of circumstances, and that punish-
> ment was consequently a violation of justice.
>
> (Roe 1988: 132)

Godwin argued that human beings act in line with reason and
that it was impossible for them to be rationally persuaded by an

argument without their conduct being regulated accordingly. Reason, for Godwin, encouraged benevolence. 'Truth', he wrote in *Political Justice*, 'is omnipotent: The vices and moral weakness of man are not invincible: Man is perfectible, or in other words susceptible of perpetual improvement' (Godwin 1985: 140). Godwin's optimistic rationalism would not entirely satisfy Wordsworth for very long. Already in *Adventures on Salisbury Plain*, which like *Salisbury Plain* remained unpublished, Wordsworth shows his concern with areas of the human mind that escape the pale of reason: above all in the sailor's guilty suffering, remorse and despair. Nevertheless, Wordsworth found in Godwin points of contact with his own radical indignation at the workings of contemporary society.

Something like radical sentiment is also apparent in Coleridge's early writing. In a very early poem, 'Destruction of the Bastille', written possibly in 1789, Coleridge rhapsodized on the destruction of the famous prison fortress by the Paris revolutionaries on 14 July 1789. This poem is full of rather conventional liberal abstractions. It does not pay detailed attention to the material circumstances of the oppressed. Nor does it attend to the hard facts of the revolutionary processes by which the oppressed throw off the oppressors. All we have is, in the fifth stanza, a sentimentally idealized peasant watching his crops grow:

> But cease, ye pitying bosoms, cease to bleed!
>   Such scenes no more demand the tear humane;
> I see, I see! glad Liberty succeed
>   With every patriot virtue in her train!
>     And mark yon peasant's raptur'd eyes;
>     Secure he views his harvests rise;
>     No fetter vile the mind shall know,
>     And Eloquence shall fearless glow.
> Yes! Liberty the soul of Life shall reign,
> Shall throb in every pulse, shall flow thro' every vein!

> (21–30; Coleridge 1912: I. 11)

But even such a juvenile work as this indicates the tenor of Coleridge's sympathies during the early days of the Revolution. A few years later Coleridge would join with Robert Southey in proposing to set up an egalitarian commune – a Pantisocracy – in New England. The scheme was perhaps more a utopian fantasy than a realistic plan and it came to nothing. But again, the idea is symptomatic of the apparently radical drift of the young Coleridge's mind.

Radical sympathy is again apparent in Walter Savage Landor's (1775–1864) *Gebir*, which was probably begun in 1796 and published in 1798. In this long poem of seven books, which 'derives its overall structure' from classical models, particularly 'Homeric and Virgilian epic' (Hanley 1981: xviii), Gebir, a Spanish prince, invades Egypt. Charoba, the young queen of Egypt, attempting to resist Gebir, enlists the assistance of the sorceress Dalica. But when Charoba and Gebir meet, their mutual hostility turns into love. The problem is that Charoba does not tell Dalica of her change of heart and when Charoba and Gebir marry, Dalica assumes it to be merely a necessary stratagem on Charoba's part and she arranges for Gebir to be poisoned. The poem ends with the death of Gebir in the arms of the desolate Charoba. There is another, happier, story pursued in the poem. Gebir's brother, Tamar, has fallen in love with a sea nymph and following their marriage, which precedes that of Gebir and Charoba, they leave Egypt, the sea nymph showing to Tamar a vision of the great future awaiting their descendants in the European territories lying between the Rhine and the Garonne; that is, in France. It is France that is important here, for Landor was from his youth 'what he remained to the end of his days, an ardent republican and foe to kings' (Colvin 1881: 12). Landor, with all his Neoclassical taste, was an enthusiastic supporter of the French revolutionary cause and even after that cause had degenerated he did not give up on the original revolutionary principles: 'it was France only, and not the Revolution, that Landor held guilty' (Colvin 1881: 33). *Gebir*, for all its fantastic and historically remote elements, is a work which holds dear the ideals of the Revolution. 'The message . . . of *Gebir*', Sidney Colvin observes, 'is mainly political and philanthropic':

> The tragic end of the hero and his bride is designed to point a moral against the enterprises of hatred and ambition, the happy fates of Tamar and the nymph to illustrate the reward that awaits the peaceful. The progeny whom the latter pair see in a vision celebrating the triumphs of liberty are intended to symbolize the people of revolutionary France.
>
> (Colvin 1881: 28)

A passage from that vision, at the very end of the sixth book of *Gebir*, epitomizes Landor's idealism:

> Captivity led captive, War o'erthrown,
> They shall o'er Europe, shall o'er Earth extend
> Empire that seas alone and skies confine,
> And glory that shall strike the crystal stars.
>
> (VI. 305–308; Wheeler 1937: I. 47)

The humanitarian sentiment apparent in *Lyrical Ballads* is not in itself, then, a revolutionary new phenomenon, not something that marks the beginning of a new age. It has some roots in the social concerns of poets as far back as the 1770s: Oliver Goldsmith's *The Deserted Village* (1770), for example, or John Langhorne's *The Country Justice* (1774–77). But most significantly it emerges from the heated radical movement of the early 1790s, a movement in which Wordsworth and Coleridge themselves had a small part; it emerges from the continuation of radical and humanitarian sentiment throughout the decade and which received some expression, as Robert Mayo has noted, in the magazines and journals of the time. A similar point can be made about the emphasis on 'nature' in *Lyrical Ballads*.

## NATURE

A reader in the late eighteenth century would regard as 'perfectly normal a miscellany of . . . moral and philosophic poems inspired by physical nature, and lyrical pieces in a variety of kinds describing rural scenes . . . and a simple life in the out-of-doors' (Mayo 1954: 490). A sense of the health and integrity of the life of nature, in contrast with the depredations wrought by humanity, is exemplified in *Lyrical Ballads* by Wordsworth's 'Lines written in early spring':

> I heard a thousand blended notes,
> While in a grove I sate reclined,
> In that sweet mood when pleasant thoughts
> Bring sad thoughts to the mind.
>
> To her fair works did nature link
> The human soul that through me ran;
> And much it griev'd my heart to think
> What man has made of man.
>
> . . .
>
> The budding twigs spread out their fan,
> To catch the breezy air;
> And I must think, do all I can,
> That there was pleasure there.
>
> If I these thoughts may not prevent,
> If such be of my creed the plan,
> Have I not reason to lament
> What man has made of man?
>
> (1–8, 17–24; Brett and Jones 1976: 69)

This kind of contrast between the peace and fulness of nature and the evil generated by and between human beings is not, Mayo observes, innovative but a 'fulfillment of an already stale convention' (Mayo 1954: 491). He provides a 'representative list of "Wordsworthian" titles from the magazines of 1788–1798' – titles such as 'The Delights of a Still Evening', 'On the Return to the Country', or 'Description of a Morning in May' (Mayo 1954: 490). He adds that

> Underneath many of the 'nature' poems of the magazines is the familiar conviction that nature is beautiful and full of joy; that man is corrupted by civilization; that God may be found in nature; and that the study of nature not only brings pleasure, therefore, but generates moral goodness.
>
> (Mayo 1954: 490)

Nor is it only in the magazines that such 'Wordsworthian' sentiments are to be found. They are present in volumes of poetry published in the same period. To take one example: in 1793 Charlotte Smith published a blank verse poem entitled *The Emigrants*, that dealt with exiled victims of the French Revolution, which by 1793 had mutated into the Reign of Terror. In the First Book of *The Emigrants* Smith invokes a divine power that directs the movements of nature, blames 'Man' himself for spoiling his own experience of the world and expresses a desire to escape 'Society' and find solace amidst natural scenes:

> He, whose Spirit into being call'd
> This wond'rous World of Waters; He who bids
> The wild wind lift them till they dash the clouds,
> And speaks to them in thunder; or whose breath,
> Low murmuring o'er the gently heaving tides,
> When the fair Moon, in summer night serene,
> Irradiates with long trembling lines of light
> Their undulating surface; that great Power,
> Who, governing the Planets, also knows
> If but a Sea-Mew falls, whose nest is hid

> In these incumbent cliffs; He surely means
> To us, his reasoning Creatures, whom He bids
> Acknowledge and revere his awful hand,
> Nothing but good: Yet Man, misguided Man,
> Mars the fair work that he was bid enjoy,
> And makes himself the evil he deplores . . .
> How often do I half abjure Society,
> And sigh for some lone Cottage, deep embower'd
> In the green woods, that these steep chalky Hills
> Guard from the strong South West; where round their base
> The Beach wide flourishes, and the light Ash
> With slender leaf half hides the thymy turf! –
>
> (l. 19–34, 42–47; Curran 1993a: 136)

In *Lyrical Ballads* Coleridge, as well as Wordsworth, shows a 'Romantic' antipathy towards society, and celebrates in contrast, the uncorrupted nature of 'nature'. In 'The Nightingale' he thinks of the associations of melancholy that have been built up by poets around the song of the nightingale and which are falsely perpetuated by human beings in society. He rejects the artifice of these associations, seeing them as a symptom of the artifice of society, and prefers instead to contemplate the bird as a purely natural object, unencumbered by corrupting human fiction:

> some night-wandering Man, whose heart was pierc'd
> With the remembrance of a grievous wrong . . .
> First nam'd these notes a melancholy strain;
> And many a poet echoes the conceit,
> Poet, who hath been building up the rhyme
> When he had better far have stretch'd his limbs
> Beside a brook in mossy forest-dell
> By sun or moonlight, to the influxes
> Of shapes and sounds and shifting elements
> Surrendering his whole spirit, of his song
> And of his fame forgetful! so his fame

> Should share in nature's immortality,
> A venerable thing! and so his song
> Should make all nature lovelier, and itself
> Be lov'd, like nature! – But 'twill not be so;
> And youths and maidens most poetical
> Who lose the deep'ning twilights of the spring
> In ball-rooms and hot theatres, they still
> Full of meek sympathy must heave their sighs
> O'er Philomela's pity-pleading strains.
> My Friend, and my Friend's Sister! we have learnt
> A different lore: we may not thus profane
> Nature's sweet voices always full of love
> And joyance!
>
> (16–17, 22–43; Brett and Jones 1976: 41–42)

But Coleridge's expression of such sentiments was not, any more than Wordsworth's, entirely original. A comparable contrast between the insincerity of society and the pure reality of nature appears in a passage in Charlotte Smith's *The Emigrants*:

> As one, who long
> Has dwelt amid the artificial scenes
> Of populous City, deems that splendid shows,
> The Theatre, and pageant pomp of Courts,
> Are only worth regard; forgets all taste
> For Nature's genuine beauty; in the lapse
> Of gushing waters hears no soothing sound,
> Nor listens with delight to sighing winds,
> That, on their fragrant pinions, waft the notes
> Of birds rejoicing in the tangled copse;
> Nor gazes pleas'd on Ocean's silver breast,
> While lightly o'er it sails the summer clouds
> Reflected in the wave, that, hardly heard,
> Flows on the yellow sands.
>
> (I. 260–73; Curran 1993a: 144–45)

The most remarkable 'nature' poem in *Lyrical Ballads* and one which is sometimes taken to exemplify the character of the Romantic rebellion against traditional poetic modes is Wordsworth's 'Lines written a few miles above Tintern Abbey'. Of 'Tintern Abbey', however, Mayo writes:

> it must have seemed in its day far from revolutionary. Only two of the nine notices of the first edition mentioned it at all. . . . Southey in the *Critical* and Dr. Burney in the *Monthly Review*. . . . there was no sign of surprise or bewilderment. To Southey the poem seemed supremely normal. . . . Dr. Burney described it as 'The reflections of no common mind; poetical, beautiful, and philosophical'. He objected, it is true, to the pernicious primitivism of the poem. But this was no novelty in 1798, and there is no indication that he regarded the poem as otherwise aberrant. With good reason – for, as we know, 'poetical, beautiful, and philosophical' verses written in connection with particular regions and landscapes were one of the commonest species of poetry, in the magazines and outside. For more than half a century popular poets had been evoking in a wide variety of metrical forms, roughly equivalent 'wild green landscapes' and 'secluded scenes', and then reflecting upon them in the philosophic manner of *Tintern Abbey*. . . . Regarded solely in terms of the modes of eighteenth-century topographical poetry, surely *Tintern Abbey* is one of the most conventional poems in the whole volume.
>
> (Mayo 1954: 492–93)

'Tintern Abbey' certainly falls broadly within the long-established genre of topographical poetry – a genre which goes back at least as far as Sir John Denham's *Cooper's Hill* (1642) and which was widely practised throughout the eighteenth century by poets such John Dyer, who published *Grongar Hill*, a poem describing the scenery of the river Towy, in 1726; or Richard Jago, who published *Edge Hill*, describing views across the county of Warwickshire, in

1767. But while 'Tintern Abbey' might in some respects be conventional in terms of *some* of the modes of eighteenth-century topographical poetry, it is not so in terms of all of them. In 1713 Alexander Pope published a topographical poem entitled *Windsor Forest*, where we learn that

> Here Hills and Vales, the Woodland and the Plain,
> Here Earth and Water seem to strive again,
> Not *Chaos*-like together crush'd and bruis'd,
> But as the World, harmoniously confused:
> Where Order in Variety we see,
> And where, tho' all things differ, all agree . . .
> There, interspers'd in Lawns and opening Glades,
> Thin Trees arise that shun each other's shades.
> Here in full Light the russet Plains extend;
> There, wrapt in Clouds the bluish Hills ascend . . .
> Not proud *Olympus* yields a nobler Sight,
> Tho' Gods assembled grace his tow'ring Height,
> Than what more humble Mountains offer here,
> Where, in their Blessings, all those Gods appear.
> See *Pan* with Flocks, with Fruits *Pomona* crowned,
> Here blushing *Flora* paints th'enamell'd ground . . .
> Rich Industry sits smiling on the plains,
> And Peace and Plenty tell, a STUART reigns.
>
> (11–16, 21–4, 33–8, 41–2; Audra and Williams 1961: 149–52)

This sort of description has very little to do with nature itself and a great deal to do with humankind and society. Nature, here, is ruthlessly arranged. The essential composition is, like that in a certain type of painting, made up of foreground, middle-distance and background ('There . . . /Thin Trees arise . . . /Here . . . the russet Plains extend;/There . . . the bluish Hills ascend'). In the Neoclassical diction of the passage there is no attempt to engage directly with natural detail. Instead, the lines abound in generalization and in classical allusion and personification. In fact, nature doesn't really even exist in this passage except as a token of the social values of order and prosperity. The stance of the viewer of nature is, similarly, accommodated entirely to the social order that he is interested in eulogizing ('Peace and Plenty tell, a STUART reigns'). There is, indeed, no 'I' in the passage – the 'I' of the viewer is subsumed by the collective 'we' in the fifth line. The subjectivity of the individual does not intrude as a subject or theme of the verse. This kind of topographical writing not only has little or nothing to do with physical nature, it has little or nothing to do with what Wordsworth made of the topographical genre in 'Tintern Abbey'. It is the type of poetry against which Wordsworth's Romantic 'rebellion' is sometimes measured.

In 'Tintern Abbey' nature is, in fact, arranged as fiercely as it is in 'Windsor Forest'. But the principles of the arrangement are radically different. Not only is there no classical allusion and personification but the presentation of nature is structured according to the inward motions and transitions of the observing consciousness. The thoughts, reflections and memories of the individual mind are the subject and theme of this verse and nature becomes a token of – is assimilated to the representation of – those thoughts, reflections and memories. Individual subjectivity and nature are, moreover, transcendentalized: they are attributed a spiritual dimension that is greater than the merely individual and the material. Nature is important insofar as it manifests the same transcendental energy as informs the human mind and at the same time provides an objective, material barrier which allows the individual subject to recognize transcendence without being overwhelmed by it ('A motion and a spirit, that impels/All thinking things, all objects of all thought'):

> Five years have passed; five summers, with the length
> Of five long winters! and again I hear
> These waters, rolling from their mountain-springs
> With a sweet inland murmur . . .

Though absent long,
These forms of beauty have not been to me,
As is a landscape to a blind man's eye:
But oft, in lonely rooms, and mid the din
Of towns and cities, I have owed to them,
In hours of weariness, sensations sweet,
Felt in the blood, and felt along the heart,
And passing even into my purer mind
With tranquil restoration . . .
And now, with gleams of half-extinguish'd thought,
With many recognitions dim and faint,
And somewhat of a sad perplexity,
The picture of the mind revives again:
While here I stand, not only with the sense
Of present pleasure, but with pleasing thoughts
That in this moment there is life and food
For future years. And so I dare to hope
Though changed, no doubt, from what I was, when first
I came among these hills; when like a roe
I bounded o'er the mountains, by the sides
Of the deep rivers, and the lonely streams,
Wherever nature led; more like a man
Flying from something that he dreads, than one
Who sought the thing he loved . . .
                    For I have learned
To look on nature, not as in the hour
Of thoughtless youth, but hearing oftentimes
The still, sad music of humanity . . .
                    And I have felt
A presence that disturbs me with the joy
Of elevated thoughts; a sense sublime
Of something far more deeply interfused,
Whose dwelling is the light of setting suns,
And the round ocean, and the living air,

And the blue sky, and in the mind of man,
A motion and a spirit, that impels
All thinking things, all objects of all thought,
And rolls through all things. Therefore am I still
A lover of the meadows and the woods,
And mountains . . .
      well pleased to recognize
In nature and the language of the sense,
The anchor of my purest thoughts, the nurse,
The guide, the guardian of my heart, and soul
Of all my moral being.

(1–4, 23–31, 59–73, 89–92, 94–105, 108–12;
Brett and Jones 1976: 113–16)

It is this kind of focus on and celebration of subjectivity that is sometimes seen as the distinctive Romantic innovation. But while the 'extreme assertion of the self' (Drabble 1985: 842) and the use of nature 'as a stimulus for the poet to engage in the most characteristic human activity, that of thinking' (Abrams 1993: 128) are crucial features of Romantic writing, they didn't suddenly appear with the publication of *Lyrical Ballads* in 1798.

Between 1726 and 1730 James Thomson published a poem in four books entitled *The Seasons*, a work certainly known by Wordsworth. In this poem nature is understood as an expression of divine force ('Th'informing Author in his Works appears', ('Spring', 860; Sambrook 1981: 42)) and Thomson's moral reflections often give the impression not of being imposed on nature from the outside – of being simply appended to straightforward descriptions of nature – but of deriving intrinsically from the contemplation of nature. As Thomson's 1726 Preface to 'Winter' puts it:

> I know no Subject ... more ready to awake the poetical Enthusiasm, the philosophical Reflection, and the moral Sentiment, than the *Works of Nature*. Where can we meet with

> such Variety, such Beauty, such Magnificence? All that
> enlarges, and transports, the Soul?
>
> (Sambrook 1981: 305)

At times Thomson registers the way in which nature stirs in the
human observer feelings of delighted awe:

> Shook sudden from the Bosom of the Sky,
> A thousand Shapes or glide athwart the Dusk,
> Or stalk majestic on. Deep-rous'd, I feel
> A sacred Terror, a severe Delight,
> Creep thro' my mortal frame.
>
> ('Summer', 538–42; Sambrook 1981: 86)

At times nature calms the human heart:

> by the vocal Woods and Waters lull'd,
> And lost in lonely Musing, in a Dream,
> Confus'd, of careless Solitude, where mix
> Ten thousand wandering Images of Things,
> Soothe every Gust of Passion into Peace,
> All but the Swellings of the soften'd Heart,
> That waken, not disturb the tranquil Mind.
>
> ('Spring', 460–66; Sambrook 1981: 24)

Thomson established a taste for descriptions of the life in nature
that lasted throughout the century, from Joseph Warton's *The
Enthusiast: or the Lover of Nature* (1744), through James Beattie's
*The Minstrel; or, the Progress of Genius* (1771–74) and William
Cowper's *The Task* (1785), to that predilection for 'subjects drawn
from nature' which Robert Mayo describes as 'commonplace in
the minor verse of the last years of the eighteenth century' (Mayo
1954: 490) and which formed, in part, the context within which
the *Lyrical Ballads* were composed.

Thomson's *Seasons* – with its paean to 'Inspiring GOD! who
boundless Spirit all,/ . . . pervades,/Adjusts, sustains, and agitates

the Whole' ('Spring', 853–55; Sambrook 1981: 42) – lies behind 'Tintern Abbey' with its 'sense sublime/Of something far more deeply interfused'. So, too, do the works by Warton, Beattie and Cowper. In *The Enthusiast: or the Lover of Nature* Joseph Warton, as Beattie and Cowper after him, showed himself a poet of what is sometimes called the 'Age of Sensibility'. The term defines writers in the period roughly following the death of Pope (1744) through to the publication of *Lyrical Ballads* whose tastes contrasted with the broad maintenance of early eighteenth-century Neoclassical values in the writings of contemporaries such as Dr Johnson. It defines what used to be called a 'pre-Romantic' stirring – found also in the works of writers such as William Collins (1721–59) and Christopher Smart (1722–71) – against the authoritative ethos of the time.

Philosophically, the ancestry of the 'Age of Sensibility' is often traced back to the Earl of Shaftesbury, who collected his main writings in *Characteristics of Men, Manners, Opinions, and Times*, which was first published in 1711. Shaftesbury reacted against the views of the seventeenth-century philosopher Thomas Hobbes, the author of *Leviathan* (1651), who had held that human beings are motivated above all else by self-interest. Shaftesbury stressed that human beings have 'affections', both for themselves and for the creatures around them. Benevolence, founded in this capacity for 'affections' and the ability to sympathize profoundly with the sorrows and joys of one's fellows, was asserted by Shaftesbury as an innate human characteristic. This kind of emphasis on the 'affections' was one strand of thought feeding into the broadly humanitarian sympathies of writers of the 'Age of Sensibility'. It was an age characterized, then, by a recoil from early eighteenth-century Neoclassical 'correctness' towards a stress on spontaneity, towards an emphasis on humanitarian values and on the idea of original genius and the importance of the imagination. It was characterized by an admiration of the sublime as that power in nature and art which inspires awe and deep emotion and which is manifest in grand and wild natural scenes and in the writings of older, native British writers who did not subscribe to the early eighteenth-century Neoclassical proprieties (I shall comment in more detail on the idea of the sublime in the final chapter). Instead of Classical writers such as Virgil, Horace and Ovid there was a turn to models such as Spenser, Shakespeare and Milton. And along with these models came an interest in ballads, folk literature and mediaeval romance.

Two writers who exemplified this latter interest and whose works were popular and highly influential were Thomas Percy, who published his *Reliques of Ancient English Poetry* in 1765, and James Macpherson who, in the 1760s, published highly individual 'translations' of poetry by the ancient Gaelic bard, Ossian. The taste for the exceptional rather than the conformable also revealed itself in vogues for the Oriental and the Gothic – in works such as William Beckford's *Vathek* (1786), Horace Walpole's *The Castle of Otranto* (1765), Ann Radcliffe's *The Mysteries of Udolpho* (1794), and M.G. Lewis' *The Monk* (1796). This liking for the thrills of unusual and uncharted psychological territories was similarly apparent in the dwelling on mystery and melancholy that typified what has been called 'the poetry of night and tombs' (Tieghem 1930: 3): poems, that is, like Edward Young's *The Complaint, or Night Thoughts on Life, Death and Immortality* (1742–45) and Robert Blair's *The Grave* (1743).

The move towards interior rather than exterior points of reference that is apparent in the Gothic or the 'Graveyard' type of writing is paralleled in the emotionalism of Thomas Gray's 1742 'Sonnet [on the Death of Mr Richard West]'. Here we find Gray complaining: 'My lonely anguish melts no heart but mine;/ . . . I fruitless mourn to him that cannot hear,/And weep the more because I weep in vain' (7, 13–14; Lonsdale 1969: 67–68). An interior orientation also defines the naked enthusiasm of Joseph Warton in *The Enthusiast: or the Lover of Nature*, where enthusiasm is as much the subject of the verse as nature:

> All-beauteous Nature! by thy boundless charms
> Oppress'd, O, where shall I begin thy praise,
> Where turn th'ecstatic eye, how ease my breast
> That pants with wild astonishment and love!
>
> (145–48; Warton 1822: 261)

In addition to such poetry of fervour, Warton published a critical study, *An Essay on the Writings and Genius of Pope* (1st vol: 1756; 2nd vol: 1782), which contrasts poets of the 'sublime and pathetic' with 'men of wit, and men of sense' (Warton 1756: xi, iv). The latter and lower category includes the early eighteenth-century Neoclassical productions of Pope, while the former and greater embraces the work of Spenser, Shakespeare and Milton: 'WIT and SATIRE are transitory and perishable, but NATURE and PASSION are eternal' (Warton 1756: 334). Warton's feeling for feeling helped prepare the ground for Wordsworth's poetry, as did James Beattie's *The Minstrel,* a poem in Spenserian stanzas which traces, in the words of Beattie's Preface, 'the progress of a Poetical Genius . . . from the first dawning of fancy and reason' (Beattie 1831: 3). In this poem the protagonist Edwin, a solitary and pensive boy, finds his education in wandering amidst natural scenes. This wandering, which is the structural principle of what can at times seem like a shapeless and rambling poem, nevertheless betokens a consciousness of self that looks forward to Wordsworth. Likewise William Cowper developed a poetry of introspection which fused observation of natural scenes with a record of the fluxes and refluxes of the mind, in a way that prefigures 'Tintern Abbey':

> Again the harmony comes o'er the vale;
> And through the trees I view th'embattled tow'r
> Whence all the music. I again perceive
> The soothing influence of the wafted strains,
> And settle in soft musings as I tread
> The walk, still verdant, under oaks and elms,
> Whose outspread branches overarch the glade.
>
> (*The Task,* vi. 65–71; I'Anson Fausset 1931: 406)

If poets of this type stressed the relationship between mind and nature in a way that prepared the ground for Wordsworth, then another poet, Mark Akenside, specifically stressed what was to become a key Romantic term – imagination – in his exploration of the relations between mind and nature. Akenside wrote a poem entitled *The Pleasures of Imagination* which he first published in 1744 and which was then republished in a revised form in 1772. In the first book of the 1744 version Akenside sees nature as the actualization of divine imagining:

> Ere the radiant sun
> Sprang from the east . . .
> Then liv'd the almighty One: then, deep-retir'd
> In his unfathom'd essence, view'd the forms,
> The forms eternal of created things;
> The radiant sun, the moon's nocturnal lamp . . .
> From the first
> Of days, on them his love divine he fix'd,
> His admiration: till in time compleat,
> What he admir'd and lov'd, his vital smile
> Unfolded into being. Hence the breath
> Of life informing each organic frame,
> Hence the green earth, and wild resounding waves.
>
> (I. 59–60, 64–67, 69–75; Akenside 1772: 13–14)

Akenside emphasizes how the human imagination is stimulated into activity ('discloses every tuneful spring') by the divinely inspired forms of nature:

> even so did Nature's hand
> To certain species of external things,
> Attune the finer organs of the mind:
> So the glad impulse of congenial powers,
> Or of sweet sound, or fair-proportion'd form,
> The grace of motion, or the bloom of light,
> Thrills through imagination's tender frame,

From nerve to nerve: all naked and alive
They catch the spreading rays: till now the soul
At length discloses every tuneful spring,
To that harmonious movement from without
Responsive.

(I. 113–24; Akenside 1772: 16)

It is, indeed, an interaction, since the divine energy manifest in nature is found also within the human mind, which is seen as being driven to be *active* on analogy with the divine mind:

the mind . . .
appeals to nature, to the winds
And rowling waves, the sun's unwearied course,
The elements and seasons: all declare
For what the eternal maker has ordain'd
The powers of man: we feel within ourselves
His energy divine: he tells the heart . . .
to be great like him,
Beneficent and active. Thus the men
Whom nature's works can charm, with God himself
Hold converse.

(III. 613, 620–25, 628–31; Akenside 1772: 100–101)

In book four of the 1772 version of *The Pleasures of Imagination* Akenside records how the numinous awe he felt as a child amidst the scenes of nature remains, even in adulthood, the master-light of all his seeing:

O ye Northumbrian shades, which overlook
The rocky pavement and the mossy falls
Of solitary Wensbeck's limpid stream;
How gladly I recall your well-known seats
Belov'd of old, and that delightful time
When all alone, for many a summer's day,
I wander'd through your calm recesses, led

In silence by some powerful hand unseen.
  Nor will I e'er forget you; nor shall e'er
The graver tasks of manhood, or the advice
Of vulgar wisdom, move me to disclaim
Those studies which possess'd me in the dawn
Of life, and fix'd the color of my mind
For every future year: whence even now
From sleep I rescue the clear hours of morn,
And, while the world around lies overwhelm'd
In idle darkness, am alive to thoughts
Of honourable fame, of truth divine
Or moral.

(IV. 38–56; Akenside 1772: 220–21)

These lines anticipate Wordsworth so distinctively that in 1926, in his Preface to a collection of eighteenth-century verse, David Nichol Smith asked his readers to guess who it was that wrote them: 'Not Wordsworth, but Akenside' (Nichol Smith, 1926: x).

Yet Akenside does not go as far as some of the Romantics later would in finding images which suggest the autonomous activity, the self-sufficient creativity, of the imagination. In his famous book *The Mirror and the Lamp* M.H. Abrams has studied the contrast between what he terms the Neoclassic view of art as imitation and the Romantic view of art as expression. In the eighteenth-century Neoclassicism of the 'Age of Johnson', he observes,

we find standards for art running the gamut from a primary emphasis on typicality, generality, and 'large appearances', to the unqualified recommendation of particularity, uniqueness, and a microscopic depiction of detail. For our purpose, however, it is important to note that these discussions and disagreements took place mainly within a single aesthetic orientation. Whether art is to represent a composite of scattered beauties, generic humanity, average forms, and familiar appearances, or whether unique characteristics, undiscovered particularities, and ultra-violet discriminations – all these forms and qualities are conceived to be inherent in the constitution of the external world, and the work of art continues to be regarded as a kind of reflector, though a selective one. The artist himself is often envisioned as the agent holding the mirror up to nature.

(Abrams 1953: 41–42)

However, it is the lamp that sheds light on the world, rather than the mirror that merely reflects it, that is for Abrams the characteristic metaphor of the Romantic expressivist view of the artist and his or her art:

the central tendency of the expressive theory may be summarized in this way: A work of art is essentially the internal made external, resulting from a creative process operating under the impulse of feeling, and embodying the combined product of the poet's perceptions, thoughts, and feelings. The primary source and subject matter of a poem, therefore, are the attributes and actions of the poet's own mind; or if aspects of the external world, then these only as they are converted from fact to poetry by the feelings and operations of the poet's mind. . . . The paramount cause of poetry is not . . . as in neo-classic criticism, a final cause, the effect intended upon the audience; but instead an efficient cause – the impulse within the poet of feelings and desires seeking expression, or the compulsion of the 'creative' imagination which, like God the creator, has its internal source of motion.

(Abrams 1953: 22)

'The change from imitation to expression, and from the mirror to the fountain, the lamp, and related analogues, was not', Abrams continues, 'an isolated phenomenon':

It was an integral part of a corresponding change in popular epistemology – that is, in the concept of the role played by the mind in perception which was current among romantic poets and critics. . . . John Locke [1632–1704] – who more than any philosopher established the stereotype for the popular view of the mind in the eighteenth century – was able to levy upon a long tradition of ready-made parallels in giving definition to his view of the mind in perception as a passive receiver for images presented ready-formed from without. The mind in Locke's *Essay* [*Concerning Human Understanding*, 1690] is said to resemble a mirror which fixes the objects it reflects. Or . . . it is a *tabula rasa* on which sensations write or paint themselves. . . .

The analogies for the mind in the writings of both Wordsworth and Coleridge show a radical transformation. Varied as these are, they usually agree in picturing the mind in perception as active rather than inertly receptive, and as contributing to the world in the very process of perceiving the world.

(Abrams 1953: 57–58)

A number of Romantic writers may be found suggesting the idea of the mind's contribution, at least in some degree, to experience. Beneath the frontispiece to William Blake's 'For the Sexes: The Gates of Paradise' (first published 1793), for example, appeared the couplet: 'The Suns Light when he unfolds it/Depends on the Organ that beholds it' (Erdman and Bloom 1970: 257). In *The Prelude*, Wordsworth asserted the mind's creativity in perception when, speaking of the growing child, he wrote:

Emphatically such a being lives,
An inmate of this *active* universe.
From Nature largely he receives, nor so
Is satisfied, but largely gives again;
For feeling has to him imparted strength,
And – powerful in all sentiments of grief,
Of exultation, fear and joy – his mind,
Even as an agent of the one great mind,
Creates, creator and receiver both,

Working but in alliance with the works
Which it beholds.

(1805, II. 265–75; Wordsworth, Abrams and Gill 1979: 78, 80)

Coleridge, likewise, commented in a poem of 1802, that 'we receive but what we give,/And in our life alone does Nature live' ('Dejection: An Ode', 47–48; Coleridge 1912: I. 365).

The idea that the mind constitutes, at least to some extent, what it perceives is generally not taken to be part of a subjectivist and solipsistic epistemology. A number of Romantic writers suggest that the mind possesses a faculty which enables it to see through the forms of the material world to a greater, spiritual reality behind it. In an 1810 commentary on one of his own paintings, 'A Vision of the Last Judgement', Blake spoke of such a visionary faculty as something distinct from the mechanisms of ordinary perception:

> The Nature of Visionary Fancy or Imagination is very little Known & the Eternal nature & permanence of its ever Existent Images is considerd as less permanent than the things of Vegetative & Generative Nature yet the Oak dies as well as the Lettuce but Its Eternal Image & Individuality never dies. . . . I assert for My self that I do not behold the Outward Creation & that to me it is hindrance & not Action it is as the Dirt upon my feet No part of Me. What it will be Questiond When the Sun rises do you not see a round Disc of fire somewhat like a Guinea O no no I see an Innumerable company of the Heavenly host crying Holy Holy Holy is the Lord God Almighty I question not my Corporeal or Vegetative Eye any more than I would Question a Window concerning a Sight I look thro it & not with it.

(Erdman and Bloom 1970: 544–45, 555)

In his 'Ode: Intimations of Immortality From Recollections of Early Childhood' (first published 1807) Wordsworth regrets the passing of a childhood state when the immortal origins of the soul seemed everywhere apparent:

> Our birth is but a sleep and a forgetting:
> The Soul that rises with us, our life's Star,
>     Hath had elsewhere its setting,
>       And cometh from afar:
>     Not in entire forgetfulness,
>     And not in utter nakedness,
> But trailing clouds of glory do we come
>       From God, who is our home:
> Heaven lies about us in our infancy!
>
> (58–66; Gill 1984: 299)

We learn that though their initial brilliance has faded those early visions of the 'eternal mind' (113; Gill 1984: 300) still hold a constitutive authority over the human adult's mind. They are

> yet the fountain light of all our day,
> Are yet a master light of all our seeing;
>     Uphold us, cherish us, and make
> Our noisy years seem moments in the being
> Of the eternal Silence: truths that wake,
>       To perish never.
>
> (154–59; Gill 1984: 301)

The visionary faculty is sometimes thought to partake in the very nature of ultimate reality itself. Thus, in *The Prelude*, Wordsworth could speak of the child's mind interacting with its environment 'Even as an agent of the one great mind'. In expressions such as this the individual human subject is identified with a transcendent subjectivity or spirit. This transcendent spirit is understood to lie deeper than the earthly contraries of self and other, of mind and nature, of subject and object. And within this transcendent spirit those contraries are thought to be reconciled. Subject, mind, or spirit, are given a priority over nature and matter, so that the forms of the material world may be read as emblems of a profounder, spiritual reality transcending nature, time and space. Thus it is understood that the tension between subject and object in Romantic writing is resolved in an idealist fashion through the positing of an ultimate correlation between the individual mind and the mind of the absolute. And that part or capacity of the individual mind that is founded in and has the capacity to apprehend the absolute is frequently referred to by the Romantics with the term imagination, just as the term imagination is often used to define the absolute itself. In chapter 13 of *Biographia Literaria* (1817) Coleridge spoke of the 'primary IMAGINATION' as 'the living Power and prime Agent of all human Perception . . . a repetition in the finite mind of the eternal act of creation in the infinite I AM' (Shawcross 1907: I. 202). When Wordsworth relates, in the sixth book of *The Prelude*, how the power of Imagination rose within him during a journey across the Alps, he describes it as a power which revealed all natural forces to be something like the sign-language of the absolute:

> The immeasurable height
> Of woods decaying, never to be decayed,
> The stationary blasts of waterfalls . . .
> The unfettered clouds and region of the heavens,
> Tumult and peace, the darkness and the light,
> Were all like workings of one mind, the features
> Of the same face, blossoms upon one tree,
> Characters of the great apocalypse,
> The types and symbols of eternity,
> Of first, and last, and midst, and without end.
>
> (1805, VI. 556–58, 566–72; Wordsworth, Abrams and Gill 1979: 218)

Sometimes Wordsworth refers to the 'first, and last, and midst, and without end' using the term imagination, as when he speaks in *The Prelude* of '[t]he soul, the imagination of the whole' (1805, XIII. 65; Wordsworth, Abrams and Gill 1979: 460). William Blake conflated the human and the more than human when he wrote, in his commentary on 'A Vision of the Last Judgement', that

> This world of Imagination is the World of Eternity it is the
> Divine bosom into which we shall all go after the death of the
> Vegetated body.
>
> (Erdman and Bloom 1970: 545)

*Full-blown* theoretical expositions of an idealist and expressivist theory of art were not, however, made by the Romantic poets themselves. Such an exposition, as Marilyn Butler has observed, had to wait until the 1830s – well *after* the high point of Romantic poetic expression – and the writings of Thomas Carlyle, J.S. Mill and John Keble (Butler 1981: 8). There are formulations in Wordsworth's poetry of the early nineteenth century which may be read as encapsulating the expressivist view of the artist's mind and as acclaiming the faculty of imagination as the primary, creative faculty of mind. I shall have more to say later in this book on the typically 'Romantic' idealist celebration of the imagination in relation to other supposedly typical Romantic tendencies of thought, such as political radicalism. For the moment, I would mention that the expressivist view of the artist's mind which it is possible to find in Wordsworth's poetry of the early nineteenth century is much less apparent in Wordsworth's contributions to the *Lyrical Ballads* of 1798. Even in 'Tintern Abbey' Wordsworth is still only moving towards the later expressivist or idealist position. And that movement had already been occurring in the writing of various individuals – Akenside, for example – in the eighteenth century. Sometimes the later, more fully elaborated Romantic idealist view of the imagination is read back into 'Tintern Abbey'. R.L. Brett and A.R. Jones have discussed the influence of David Hartley (1705–57) on the poems of *Lyrical Ballads*. David Hartley subscribed to that branch of philosophical thought which is termed empiricism: the idea that human concepts or knowledge come not, in some idealist sense, from within but are based on experience through the senses. Brett and Jones write that:

> Hartley was an empiricist in the tradition of Locke, but his

reputation rested on the plausibility with which he had restated in physiological terms the theory of the association of ideas. In its simplest form the theory of association stated that the order in which our ideas succeed one another is governed by the order in which the sensations (of which the ideas themselves are copies) occurred. The material of consciousness is made up, firstly, of sensations or (as modern philosophers would say) sense-data; secondly, simple ideas which are copies of sensations, or sensations which remain after the objects which cause them have been removed; and thirdly, complex ideas which are compounded of simple ideas. These three stages, as we may call them, correspond roughly to sensation, memory and thought. Within consciousness one idea will tend to call up another if the two ideas have been previously associated either in space or time and more especially so if this association has been frequently experienced. . . .

Central to Hartley's restatement of association was the notion that the mind is passive in perception, a mere *tabula rasa* upon which the outside world writes its impressions. In accordance with this strict empiricism Hartley had stressed the importance of sensation as the basis of all our knowledge, including our moral principles. Morality, on such a view, was the product of experience, built up from the effects of environment upon one's personal development. This is of central importance in much of Wordsworth's poetry. . . .

The *Preface* which Wordsworth wrote to the 1800 edition of *Lyrical Ballads* makes his debt to Hartley abundantly clear, and many of the poems bear the marks of this influence. The *Anecdote for Fathers* is a particularly good example of how ideas are associated in a state of excitement, one of the aims, it will be remembered, which Wordsworth set himself in these poems.

(Brett and Jones 1976: xxxiii–xxxv)

Brett and Jones go on to say that it would be possible to read 'Tintern Abbey' in the light of Hartleian ideas: 'Hartley's account of how the mind moves from sensation through perception to thought, is turned into an analogy of how the individual passes from childhood through youth to maturity' (Brett and Jones 1976: xxxv–xxxvi). Having suggested that 'Tintern Abbey' may be read as being informed by empiricist rather than idealist ideas, Brett and Jones go on to say, however, that

> attractive as this may be, we meet a difficulty in the lines where Wordsworth describes himself as
>
> > . . . still
> > A lover of the meadows and the woods,
> > And mountains; and of all that we behold
> > From this green earth; of all the mighty world
> > Of eye and ear, *both what they half-create,*
> > *And what perceive*; well pleased to recognize
> > In nature and the language of the sense,
> > The anchor of my purest thoughts, the nurse,
> > The guide, the guardian of my heart, and soul
> > Of all my moral being.

The phrase in italics hardly suggests the rigorous empiricism of Hartley. It suggests rather a passage in *Biographia Literaria*, written many years later, in which Coleridge is criticizing Hartley's theory, and where he writes:

> There are evidently two powers at work [in the mind], which relatively to each other are active and passive; and this is not possible without an intermediate faculty, which is at once both active and passive. (In philosophical language, we must denominate this intermediate faculty in all its degrees and determinations, the IMAGINATION . . . ).
>
> (Brett and Jones 1976: xxxvi)

But these lines of 'Tintern Abbey' are not so much of a 'difficulty' if we see them as part of a process of moving towards idealist perspectives – a process in which Wordsworth was again not an innovator but rather a late-comer. M.H. Abrams looked not to the later Coleridge on 'imagination' for a way of reading these lines but to the earlier poet to whom Wordsworth actually directed our attention:

In Wordsworth's early passage from 'Tintern Abbey',

> All the mighty world
> Of eye, and ear, – both what they half create,
> And what perceive,

the elements created in the act of perception may well be nothing more than Locke's secondary sense-qualities. Wordsworth himself draws attention in a note to the source of this passage in Young's *Night Thoughts*. Our senses, Young had said,

> Give taste to fruits; and harmony to groves;
> Their radiant beams to gold, and gold's bright fire . . .
> Our senses, as our reason, are divine
> And half create the wondrous world they see.
> But for the magic organ's powerful charm
> Earth were a rude, uncolour'd chaos still.
> Objects are th'occasion; ours th'exploit . . .
> Man makes the matchless image, man admires . . .

The reference to the secondary qualities as constituting the mind's addition to perception is here unmistakable, and brings to the fore an interesting aspect of the Lockean tradition. For though Locke had said that in acquiring the simple ideas of sense the mind, like a mirror, is passively receptive, he had gone on to make a further distinction. Some simple ideas are 'resemblances' of primary qualities which 'are in the things themselves'; but the simple ideas of secondary qualities, such as colors, sounds, smells, tastes, have no counterpart in any external body. In Locke's dualism, then, we have the view that our perception of the sensible world consists partly of elements reflecting things as they are, and partly of elements which are merely 'ideas in the mind' without 'likeness of something exist-ing without'. Locke, therefore, implicitly gave the mind a part-nership in sense-perception; what Young did was to convert this into an active partnership of 'giving,' 'making,' and 'cre-ation'. In this simple metaphoric substitution, we find Locke's sensationalism in the process of converting itself into what is often considered its epistemological opposite.

(Abrams 1953: 62–63)

The element of epistemological idealism which it may be possible to discern in 'Tintern Abbey' – that dimension of the poem which apparently asserts that human knowledge does not derive entirely from experience through the senses – thus has an ancestry going back far into the eighteenth century. And at this point I must consider in more detail the relations between the Enlightenment and the so-called 'Age of Sensibility'.

## ENLIGHTENMENT OR SENSIBILITY

The Enlightenment is conventionally seen as a European and American intellectual movement of the eighteenth century – exalting reason and the scientific method – which had its roots in seventeenth-century intellectual achievements such as the scien-tific discoveries of Sir Isaac Newton, the rationalism of Descartes and the empiricism of Francis Bacon and John Locke. It is often characterized as a movement which held that through the exercise of reason human beings could clear away the darkness of igno-rance, intolerance and prejudice, and move towards a juster and better life. It opposed reliance on tradition for tradition's sake and sought to found its vision of progress towards an ideal state on universal principles. In Britain the line of descent ran from Bacon through Locke to later eighteenth-century figures such as William

Godwin; in France from Descartes through Voltaire to Diderot and other compilers of *L'Encyclopédie*; in Germany from Leibnitz to Kant, who in 1784 saw the essence of 'enlightenment' as humankind's 'resolution and courage' to use the understanding 'without the guidance of another' (Reiss 1970: 54). In America, Benjamin Franklin, Thomas Jefferson and Thomas Paine were deeply influenced by tenets of the Enlightenment, which gave intellectual form to the American Revolution of 1775–1781, as it did a few years later to the French Revolution. It is possible to see the Enlightenment solely in terms of an exaltation of reason. Looked at this way the writers of the so-called 'Age of Sensibility', as the Romantics after them, might be seen as reacting against Enlightenment rationalism in their emphasis on the importance of feelings and their turning away from society towards the sublimities of nature. But it would be unfair to the Enlightenment to see it solely as a cold exaltation of critical intelligence. It was a more varied movement than that and, indeed, not always self-consistent.

In the first volume of his classic study *The Enlightenment: An Interpretation*, Peter Gay notes the diversity of the Enlightenment while at the same time preserving a sense of a body of similarities in thought which justifies the use of the term 'The Enlightenment':

> Synthesis demands regard for complexity: the men of the Enlightenment were divided by doctrine, temperament, environment, and generations. And in fact the spectrum of their ideas, their sometimes acrimonious disputes, have tempted many historians to abandon the search for a single Enlightenment. What, after all, does Hume, who was a conservative, have in common with Condorcet, who was a democrat? Holbach, who ridiculed all religion, with Lessing, who practically tried to invent one? Diderot, who envied and despised antiquaries, with Gibbon, who admired and emulated them? Rousseau, who worshipped Plato, with Jefferson, who could not bring himself

to finish the *Republic*? . . . These questions have their uses, but mainly as a corrective: they keep historians from sacrificing variety to unity and help to free them from simplistic interpretations that have served them for so long and so badly – interpretations that treat the Enlightenment as a compact body of doctrine, an Age of Reason, and then take the vitalism of Diderot, the passion of Rousseau, or the skepticism of Hume, as foreign bodies, as harbingers of Romanticism. This is definition by larceny; it is to strip the Enlightenment of its wealth and then complain about its poverty. . . . I shall respect the differences among the philosophes which, after all, supplied the Enlightenment with much of its vigor, generated much of its inner history. Yet, mindful that general names are not Platonic ideas but baskets collecting significant similarities, I shall speak throughout of *the* philosophes, and call the totality of their ideas, their strategies, and their careers, *the* Enlightenment, and I shall use these terms to refer to what I shall call a family, a family of intellectuals united by a single style of thinking. . . .

There were many philosophes in the eighteenth century, but there was only one Enlightenment. A loose, informal, wholly unorganized coalition of cultural critics, religious skeptics, and political reformers from Edinburgh to Naples, Paris to Berlin, Boston to Philadelphia, the philosophes made up a clamorous chorus, and there were some discordant voices among them, but what is striking is their general harmony, not their occasional discord. The men of the Enlightenment united on a vastly ambitious program, a program of secularism, humanity, cosmopolitanism, and freedom, above all, freedom in its many forms – freedom from arbitrary power, freedom of speech, freedom of trade, freedom to realize one's talents, freedom of aesthetic response, freedom, in a word, of moral man to make his own way in the world.

(Gay 1973: I. xii, 3)

Above all, Gay qualifies any view that would make a crude association between the Enlightenment and an exaltation of reason. In his second volume he observes that

> The metaphysicians of the seventeenth century had allowed their urgent desire for rationality to govern their conclusions: had not Descartes claimed, 'There is no soul so weak that it cannot, if well directed, acquire absolute power over its passions'? The philosophes thought such a claim preposterous. . . . reason, Hume insisted, neither influences the will nor gives rise to morality; nor does reason have any part in producing those associations of ideas by which men think and live. . . . He put it . . . formally in the *Treatise* [*of Human Nature*]: 'We speak not strictly and philosophically when we talk of the combat of passion and of reason. Reason is, and ought only to be the slave of the passions, and can never pretend to any other office than to serve and obey them'. . . .
>
> the limits of rational inquiry into ultimate mysteries, the impotence of reason before the passions, were . . . themes that haunted the Enlightenment. 'People ceaselessly proclaim against the passions', wrote Diderot in the opening paragraph of his first philosophical work, 'people impute to the passions all of men's pains, and forget that they are also the source of all his pleasures. It is an element of man's constitution of which we can say neither too many favorable, nor too many unfavorable things. But what makes me angry is that the passions are never regarded from any but the critical angle. People think they do reason an injury if they say a word in favor of its rivals. Yet it is only the passions, and the great passions, that can raise the soul to great things'. . . . In its treatment of the passions, as in its treatment of metaphysics, the Enlightenment was not an age of reason but a revolt against rationalism. . . .
>
> But the philosophes' revolt in psychology was also – and here its delicacy lies – a revolt against antirationalism, against

that devout psychology which meekly served Christian theology by denying man's capacity to find his own unaided way in life. ... the philosophes saw psychology as a dual escape – from unreasonable rationalism and superstitious antirationalism.

(Gay 1973: II. 187–89)

One eighteenth-century thinker who vehemently opposed 'unreasonable rationalism' was Jean-Jacques Rousseau. From his *Discourse on the Sciences and the Arts* (1751) through to *The Social Contract* (1762) Rousseau argued that two principles governed human beings in their original or natural state – a principle of self-preservation and one of compassionate revulsion at seeing their fellows suffer or die. Human beings' duties to each other derive not from their shared rationality but from their common condition as living beings. Rousseau rejected the idea that what is peculiar to human beings is their reason. The two principles governing human behaviour originate from feeling – fear at threats to individual security, on one hand, and sympathy for the situation of others, on the other. The exercise of reason belongs to the social condition of human beings. The wants of human beings in the natural state must have been simple and easily satisfied. But human beings differ from the animals in that they can exercise free choice, they can modify the pattern of their instincts and they have a capacity for improving themselves, a capacity for perfectibility. Yet this capacity means that they can fall below the animals as well as rise above them. And it is here that Rousseau's critique of contemporary civilization takes root. Rousseau sees the ownership of property as the first stage in the climb towards the civilization of his day. From ownership of property had developed all the vices, violences, inequalities, oppressions and artificialities which typified civilization as it had developed. As against a thinker like Thomas Hobbes, who had claimed that violence and viciousness were an inherent part of the depraved natural state of human beings which society sought to order and correct, Rousseau saw the natural state of human beings as having been typified by innocence and freedom which the social state had degraded. But while he praised the idea of the natural state in contrast to contemporary civilization, Rousseau saw that that natural state must have been limited. What he was arguing against was not civilization *per se*, but civilization as it had actually happened. In a famous passage from *The Social Contract* he notes:

> The passing from the state of nature to the civil society produces a remarkable change in man; it puts justice as a rule of conduct in the place of instinct, and gives his actions the moral quality they previously lacked. It is only then, when the voice of duty has taken the place of physical impulse, and right that of desire, that man, who has hitherto thought only of himself, finds himself compelled to act on other principles, and to consult his reason rather than study his inclinations. And although in civil society man surrenders some of the advantages that belong to the state of nature, he gains in return far greater ones; his faculties are so exercised and developed, his mind is so enlarged, his sentiments so ennobled, and his whole spirit so elevated that, if the abuse of his new condition did not in many cases lower him to something worse than what he had left, he should constantly bless the happy hour that lifted him forever from the state of nature and from a stupid, limited animal made a creature of intelligence and a man.
>
> (Rousseau 1968: 64–65)

Rousseau imagines a state of society where there is less separation between human beings and the innocent natural state from which they have emerged. In *Emile* (1762) he envisaged a new pattern of education which emphasizes the free, individual development of the child in the beneficial context of natural surroundings, rather than any forcing of the child to learn rules and submit to external authority. There were, of course, limitations to Rousseau's educational model in *Emile*, where he remains masculinist and anti-feminist. Nevertheless, his emphasis on the education of the feelings and his focus on the individual (albeit the male individual) as an individual, a subject to be considered in its own right distinct from social pressure, have positive aspects. These emerge posthumously both in his *Reveries of the Solitary Walker* (1782) and in his similarly autobiographical *Confessions* (1781–88). In the *Reveries* there is a tendency to assert the special spiritual disposition of certain individuals:

> there is a state where the soul can find a resting-place secure enough to establish itself and concentrate its entire being there . . . where time is nothing to it . . . no other feeling of deprivation or enjoyment, pleasure or pain, desire or fear than the simple feeling of existence, a feeling that fills our soul entirely. . . . Such is the state which I often experienced on the Island of Saint-Pierre in my solitary reveries. . . .
>
> It is true that such compensations cannot be experienced by every soul or in every situation. The heart must be at peace and its calm untroubled by any passion. The person in question must be suitably disposed and the surrounding objects conducive to his happiness.
>
> (Rousseau 1979: 88–89)

The individualism that is apparent in the *Confessions*, however, is an individualism associated with democratic and egalitarian impulses. Rousseau uses his own life as a type of general human truth and challenges the reader, suggesting that a history of the reader's own life would, in essentials, look no different. The candour of the *Confessions* may be seen as an attempt to erase the impediments that block communication or the exchange of positive feeling between individuals in the artificial conditions of civilized life. In *The Social Contract* Rousseau attacked the inequalities and oppressions of contemporary civilization, proposing instead a more equal distribution of wealth and the principle of universal justice based on equality before the law. He defined government as a contract allowing the exercise of power in agreement with the 'general will', the 'general will' being constituted by the citizens of a state, in whom sovereignty finally resides. Rousseau was not, Peter Gay writes, 'a representative figure for the Enlightenment. . . . Yet . . . [he] urged men on in the direction that the Enlightenment as a whole wanted mankind to go. . . . he did the work of the Enlightenment, and gave substance, more than any other philosophe, to the still youthful, always precarious, science of freedom' (Gay 1973: II. 552).

Although, then, rational analysis was the cardinal tenet of much Enlightenment thought, it was not advanced to the complete exclusion of feeling. Rather than insisting on the sole importance of reason it is truer to the nature of the Enlightenment in all its variety to characterize it more generally in terms of its questioning of traditional authorities, models and institutions. And while this questioning was frequently achieved by the exercise of critical intelligence, it was also conducted through asserting the value of feeling, as well as the importance of the individual subject and by proclaiming the purity and freedom of natural life in contrast with artificial, corrupt and over-rational contemporary civilization. The simultaneous emphasis on 'reason' and 'feeling' emerges often in the radical political tendency that was part of the Enlightenment's 'science of freedom'. I emphasize *part*, since not *all* Enlightenment figures were politically radical. We have, for example, seen Peter Gay contrasting the conservative David Hume with Condorcet, who was a democrat. And William Blake, who shared in the strain of Enlightenment political radicalism, was simultaneously violently opposed to the materialist and rationalist strains of the Enlightenment, as is apparent in his little poem 'Mock on, Mock on, Voltaire, Rousseau' (first published 1863). But combinations of emphases on the value of 'reason' and on the value of 'feeling' within an enlightened political radicalism were possible. In *Rights of Man*, for example, Paine defined first the rationality of claims for equal human rights before going on to speak of those claims as founded in impulses of the heart:

> in the instance of France, we see a revolution generated in the
> rational contemplation of the rights of man. . . .
>
> But Mr Burke appears to have no idea of principles, when he
> is contemplating governments. 'Ten years ago' (says he)
> 'I could have felicitated France on her having a government,
> without inquiring what the nature of that government was, or
> how it was administered'. Is this the language of a rational man?
> Is it the language of a heart feeling as it ought to feel for the
> rights and happiness of the human race?
>
> (Paine 1985: 49)

Or again, Helen Maria Williams' eulogy of the French Revolution
in her poem 'To Dr Moore . . . ' (quoted p. 27) associates
'Liberty!' with the 'light' of 'reason', but she also sees that movement towards 'Freedom' in France as driven by passion or 'ardour'
(lines 43–64).

When the Enlightenment is understood like this it is possible to
see many of the sympathies of writers of the 'Age of Sensibility' less
as subterranean, 'pre-Romantic' sympathies than as aspects of the
questioning tendency of the Enlightenment itself. And it is out of
such questioning that there emerge preoccupations which have
often been defined, misleadingly, as uniquely 'Romantic'. Take
one representative essay: Edward Young's 'Conjectures on Original
Composition', first published in 1759. In this essay Young draws a
contrast between two kinds of writer, the one kind he refers to as
'imitators' and the other, far superior, he calls 'originals'. In
praising 'originals' Young moves into a celebration of 'genius', a
power he describes, as the Romantics later were so fond of doing,
through a metaphor of organism rather than one of mechanism.
Young is extolling the virtues of individuality as he disparages
servile imitation of already established forms:

> Originals are, and ought to be, great favourites, for they
> are great benefactors; they extend the republic of letters. . . .
> Imitators only give us a sort of duplicates of what we had

... increasing the mere drug of books, while all that makes them valuable, knowledge and genius, are at a stand. ... An original may be said to be of a vegetable nature; it rises spontaneously from the vital root of genius; it grows, it is not made. Imitations are often a sort of manufacture wrought up by those mechanics, art and labour, out of pre-existent materials not their own.

(Jones 1922: 273–74)

In order that genius may be nurtured it is necessary, says Young, that two rules be observed: 'Know thyself' and 'Reverence thyself' (Jones 1922: 288–89). The emphasis here on the individual, which lies at the heart of the eulogy of genius, conjoins with an Enlightenment resistance to an unthinking, bigoted respect for tradition:

let not great examples, or authorities, browbeat thy reason into too great a diffidence of thyself: thyself so reverence, as to prefer the native growth of thy own mind to the richest import from abroad; such borrowed riches make us poor. ... The writer who neglects those two rules above will never stand alone; he makes one of a group, and thinks in wretched unanimity with the throng . . . he conceives not the least embryo of new thought; opens not the least vista through the gloom of ordinary writers, into the bright walks of rare imagination . . . while the true genius is crossing all public roads into fresh untrodden ground; he, up to the knees in antiquity, is treading the sacred footsteps of great examples, with the blind veneration of a bigot saluting the papal toe.

(Jones 1922: 289–90)

A parallel questioning of existing civilization is apparent in Joseph Warton's *The Enthusiast*. In this poem Warton manifests a distrust of established urban society with its refined arts, its businesses and law-courts, and he expresses an enthusiasm for the elemental, solitary life set against a background of wild mountains and stormy seas. It is the same sympathy for the simple, natural life as against the corruptions of contemporary civilization that surfaces in the work of such as James Beattie, William Cowper or Charlotte Smith. Enlightenment questioning of existing civilization through a eulogy of nature went hand in hand with the tendency of political radicals to word their challenge to the existing order with images of natural energy. Stephen Prickett has observed that

> in England from the very beginning many pro-Revolutionary writers had been employing images drawn from nature and the natural world, often with . . . implications of irresistible forces at work shaping human destiny. For [Thomas] Paine it forms one of the dominant images of Part II of *The Rights of Man*, which had been prepared for by earlier references to the Revolution as a new 'spring'.
>
> (Prickett 1989: 7)

In *The Enthusiast* Joseph Warton also expresses a distrust of what we might term the *Augustan* Neoclassic style. That is to say, the early eighteenth-century Neoclassicism of a writer like Pope, with his ideals of taste, polish, refinement, reason, urbanity and his style defined by the poetic couplet. It is important, here, to introduce a discrimination into the use of the term 'Neoclassical'. In a summary of Romanticism such as is given by M.H. Abrams in his *Glossary*, Neoclassicism is simply contrasted with Romanticism, which is seen as revolting against and displacing the monolithic or unitary Neoclassicism of the eighteenth century. But there was in the eighteenth century more than one Neoclassicism. The earlier phase, represented by Pope and broadly maintained in the middle and later part of the century by Samuel Johnson, held as its great authority and model the period of literary achievement under the Roman emperor Augustus (27 BC–AD 14), a period which saw the writings of Virgil, Horace and Ovid. But after the death of

Pope and in contradistinction to the values of Johnson, there was in Britain, as elsewhere in Europe, a great taste for the arts of primitive or Republican Rome. This was accompanied by a taste for the arts and supposed values of primitive Greece as against those of Athens under Pericles. And *this* Neoclassicism was a part of Enlightenment questioning of established authority. The taste for the primitively classical was part and parcel of a taste for the primitive in general, whether it was classical or mediaeval, whether it was of the dark ages or of the geographically remote. Hence there is superficial contrast but actually a deep connection between the mediaevalism of Thomas Percy, the fashion for the 'Gothic', the enthusiasm for nature, and the taste for simple, early classical forms that took hold from around the middle of the century. And while some summaries of Romanticism borrow terms from the social and political happenings of the later eighteenth century and see Romanticism as 'revolting' against Neoclassicism in general, in fact it was a version of the Neoclassical, the version which preferred primitive Greece or Republican Rome, which was the distinctive taste of those of radical tendency during the Revolutionary years. Stephen Prickett has commented on the connection that existed in France between revolution and a republican Neoclassicism:

> For many French, reared in the classical tradition that has always been a strong element in Gallic education, the appropriate model was that of Republican Rome with its suggestions of domestic virtue, stern patriotism and invincible destiny. This is an imagery made famous by, for instance, the early paintings of Jacques-Louis David, before he had become court painter to Napoleon. One thinks of *The Oath of the Horatii* (1784–85) or *Lictors returning to Brutus the Bodies of his Sons* (1789). This model not merely permitted the revolutionaries to think of themselves in terms of rugged republican virtue in defence of the mother-land, but also had the added advantage of associating the *ancien*

*régime* and its monarchist supporters with popular notions of the corruptions and degeneracy of the worst of the Roman emperors.

(Prickett 1989: 5)

In Britain the Neoclassicism that drew its inspiration from primitive Greece or Rome, with all its emphasis on simplicity and plainness of form, is apparent in William Blake's illustrations to his verse from *Songs of Innocence* in 1789 to the *Book of Los* in 1795. Primitive Neoclassicism was, in sum, a style that was associated with the revolution against the *ancien régime* or *Augustan* Neoclassicism. To characterize Romanticism as the revolutionary movement overturning Neoclassicism in general is to oversimplify what was happening in the late Enlightenment culture of Europe in the later eighteenth century.

In other words, many of the preoccupations that are frequently associated with Romanticism – a perception of the stultifying effect of an unthinking imitation of tradition, the emphasis on the political rights and the psychological capacities of the individual, the emphasis on feeling not to the exclusion of but *as well as* on reason, the emphasis on primitive simplicity and naturalness, on the importance of nature itself – were fundamentally Enlightenment preoccupations. And those emphases on 'nature' and 'simplicity', on 'humanitarianism and sentimental morality' which Robert Mayo saw in both the magazine poetry of the later eighteenth century and in the *Lyrical Ballads*, were Enlightenment emphases. The poems of *Lyrical Ballads* did not mark 'the beginning of a new age'. They were essentially compositions of the late Enlightenment. This point has best been made by Marilyn Butler in her innovative and excellent study, *Romantics, Rebels and Reactionaries*. She observes:

> Though the artists of the Enlightenment might express themselves in a variety of forms – among which homely middle-class realism was as typical as the grandest classicism – they tended

to share a number of principles. Of these the most fundamental were a rejection of the complexities of advanced society, a re-iteration of human values (often conveyed in painting, poetry and the novel by focusing upon a single central human figure), and an emphasis upon reaching out to an audience which is as wide as mankind itself. If Blake was the greatest graphic artist to employ this 'essential' style in England, Wordsworth was the greatest writer. It is as easy to miss Wordsworth's represen-tativeness as it is to miss Blake's. Both are often taken to be initiating a new artistic tradition, rather than joining an estab-lished one. Yet the fact is that Wordsworth was brought up in the mainstream of Enlightenment culture, and he realizes its potential better than any poet anywhere, with the possible exception of Goethe.

(Butler 1981: 57)

Butler also points out that the critical 'Preface' which Wordsworth attached to *Lyrical Ballads* in the second edition of 1800, a piece of writing so often taken as the manifesto of Romantic revolutionary aims, can also be seen as a document imbued with Enlightenment values:

If ever a phrase has been taken to define Romanticism in our popular notion of it, it is that part of the Preface that declares poetry to be 'the spontaneous overflow of powerful feelings'. But in its context that very sentence has Wordsworth, like a true son of the Enlightenment, putting rational thought, moral intention and social utility above the subjective, emotional side of the mind, and above the claims of self-expression. He has been writing of other kinds of poetry, both the conventional and the personal – 'false refinement and arbitrary innovation':

From such verses the Poems in these volumes will be found distinguished at least by one mark of difference, that each of them has a worthy *purpose* ... If in this opinion I am mistaken I can have little right to the name of a Poet. For

> all good poetry is the spontaneous overflow of powerful feelings:
> but though this be true, Poems to which any value can be attached,
> were never produced on any variety of subjects but by a man who
> being possessed of more than usual organic sensibility had also
> thought long and deeply. For our continued influxes of feeling
> are modified and directed by our thoughts, which are indeed the
> representatives of all our past feelings; and . . . by contemplating
> the relation of these general representatives to each other we
> discover what is really important to men.
>
> As a whole the passage stresses the controlling activity of
> the writer's intellect and moral sense. The word 'spontaneous'
> usually signifies in eighteenth-century philosophic writing not
> 'unpremeditated' but 'voluntary' or 'of one's own free will' (as
> opposed to by external constraint). That key 'Romantic' phrase
> carries a more cerebral connotation than appears at a later date.
> In its context it is moreover subordinated to purposes charac-
> teristic of the Enlightenment.
>
> (Butler 1981: 60)

Wordsworth and Coleridge's poetry of the earlier 1790s, their
*Lyrical Ballads* and Blake's early works (not to mention the writings
of Helen Maria Williams, Robert Burns, Charlotte Smith, and
others) can be seen less as part of a Romantic rebellion against the
Enlightenment than as late Enlightenment productions – the literary corollaries of politically enlightened works such as Paine's
*Rights of Man* and Wollstonecraft's *Rights of Woman*. But if the
early works of such standard Romantics as Blake, Wordsworth
and Coleridge can be seen in Enlightenment terms, what then of
the term 'Romantic'? In order to begin providing some answers to
this question it will be necessary in the next chapter to sketch
something of the history of the word and of the interpretations
designated by it.

# 2

## CONSTRUCTIONS OF
## THE TERM 'ROMANTIC'

The history of the term 'romantic' has been discussed in some detail by Logan Pearsall Smith and René Wellek, while Hans Eichner has edited a collection of essays on the topic (Smith 1925: 66–134; Wellek 1949: 1–23; Eichner 1972). In the following pages, many of my points on the earlier history of the term are drawn from these three studies.

The word 'romantic' first appeared in English in the middle of the seventeenth century (the *OED* gives 1659 as its earliest appearance). It was derived from the word *romaunt*, meaning 'romance', which had been borrowed into English from French in the middle of the sixteenth century (the *OED* gives 1530 as its earliest instance). Romance was, and is, a term used to describe mediaeval and Renaissance tales – in verse of various forms, ranging from ballad to epic – concerning knights and their chivalric exploits. And the word 'romantic', when it first appeared, described on the one hand what were perceived as the fictions of the old tales, with their enchanted castles, magicians, ogres and their representation of inflated feelings and impossible passions. The identification in the later seventeenth and eighteenth centuries of the Romantic with the chimerical was stimulated by the increasing trust in the exercise of reason as a means of establishing verifiable truth and by the appreciation of classical values and forms. Thus Thomas Shadwell, in the Preface to his play *The Sullen Lovers* (1668), displayed a Neoclassical taste for observance of the 'Three Unities' of dramatic structure and spoke disparagingly of what he termed 'Romantick' excess:

> I have in this Play, as neer as I could, observed the three Unities, of Time, Place, and Action. . . . I have endeavour'd to represent a variety of Humours . . . which was the practice of Ben Johnson [*sic*], whom I think all Dramatick Poets ought to imitate . . . he being the only person that appears to me to have made perfect Representations of Humane Life: most other Authors that I ever read . . . have wild Romantick Tales, wherein they strein Love and Honour to that Ridiculous height, that it becomes Burlesque.
>
> (Shadwell 1670: [ii]–[iii])

On the other hand, the pejorative connotations of the word 'romantic' during this period were counterbalanced by more positive associations. Joseph Addison, for example, writing in *The Spectator* in 1711 of the 'old song of Chevy-Chase . . . the favourite ballad of the common people of England', notes that 'the sentiments in that ballad are extremely natural and poetical, and full of the majestic simplicity we admire in the greatest of the ancient poets' (Jones 1922: 229, 234). He goes on to say of this ballad, which deals with the warfare between the Scots and the English, that in two of the verses the 'country of the Scotch warriors . . . has a fine romantic situation' (Jones 1922: 236). Here, in a piece praising an antique but non-classical work of art, the word 'romantic' is used positively, to conjure up an image of the picturesque and exotic. Later in the eighteenth century, in his *Letters on Chivalry and Romance* (1762), Richard Hurd spoke of what he termed the 'Gothic' literature of Elizabethan England which he contrasted with the 'classical' literature of ancient Greece and Rome. Hurd spends much time defending the poetry of Edmund Spenser, which he sees as a type of 'Gothic' literature that is not inferior to, merely different from, classical literature:

> Spenser, tho' he had been long nourished with the spirit and substance of Homer and Virgil, chose the times of chivalry for this theme, and fairy Land for the scene of his fictions. He could have planned, no doubt, an heroic design on the exact classic model: Or, he might have trimmed between the Gothic and Classic, as his contemporary Tasso did. But the charms of *fairy* prevailed. . . .
>
> Under this idea then of a Gothic, not classical poem, the *Faery Queen* is to be read and criticized. . . .
>
> When an architect examines a Gothic structure by Grecian rules, he finds nothing but deformity. But the Gothic architecture has its own rules, by which, when it comes to be examined, it is seen to have its merit, as well as the Grecian. . . .
>
> The same observation holds of the two sorts of poetry. Judge of the *Faery Queen* by the classic models, and you are shocked with its disorder: consider it with an eye to its Gothic original, and you find it regular. . . .
>
> The . . . favourable circumstance that attended [Spenser] . . . was, that he was somewhat befriended in these fictions . . . by the romantic Spirit of his age; much countenanced, and for a time brought into fresh credit, by the romantic Elizabeth. Her inclination for the fancies of Chivalry is well known.
>
> (Hurd 1762: 56, 61–62, 116)

Hurd even goes so far as to speak of 'The preeminence of the Gothic manners and fictions, as adapted to the ends of poetry, above the classic' (Hurd 1762: 76).

This kind of re-evaluation of literature which did not conform to classical proprieties – whether the mediaeval chivalric romances or Spenser's *Faerie Queen* – was developed notably by Thomas Warton in his *History of English Poetry* (1774–81). In a 'Dissertation' entitled 'Of the Origin of Romantic Fiction in Europe' which he prefixed to this work, Warton contrasts the romance or 'Romantic' literature of the middle ages and Renaissance with the literary tradition derived from classical antiquity. Throughout the 'Dissertation' he seeks to vindicate a partiality for the 'Romantic' despite its violation of classical norms and practices:

> That peculiar and arbitrary species of Fiction which we commonly call Romantic, was entirely unknown to the writers of Greece and Rome. . . . These fictions . . . seem to have centred about the eleventh century in the ideal histories of Turpin and Geoffrey of Monmouth, which record the supposititious atchievements of Charlegmagne and king Arthur, where they formed the ground-work of that species of fabulous narrative called romance. And from these beginnings or causes . . . that . . . mode of imagination arose, which at length composed the marvelous machineries of the more sublime Italian poets, and of their disciple Spenser.
>
> (Warton 1774–81: I, [1], [72])

The English use of the term 'romantic' to describe mediaeval and Renaissance writing that did not derive from classical origins passed over in the latter half of the eighteenth century into Germany. And out of this German use of the term there eventually emerged the famous distinction between the classical and the Romantic drawn by August Wilhelm Schlegel (1767–1845). René Wellek has summarized Schlegel's ideas as follows:

> In the Berlin lectures, given from 1801 to 1804, though not published until 1884, Schlegel formulated the contrast, classical and romantic, as that between the poetry of antiquity and modern

poetry, associating romantic with the progressive and Christian. He sketched a history of romantic literature which starts with a discussion of the mythology of the Middle Ages and closes with a review of the Italian poetry of what we would today call the Renaissance. Dante, Petrarch, and Boccaccio are described as the founders of modern romantic literature, though Schlegel, of course, knew that they admired antiquity. But he argued that their form and expression were totally unclassical. They did not dream of preserving the forms of antiquity in structure and composition. ... But the most important formulation was in the *Lectures* of A.W. Schlegel delivered at Vienna in 1808–09 and published in 1809–11. There romantic–classical is associated with the antithesis of organic–mechanical and plastic–picturesque. There clearly the literature of antiquity and that of neoclassicism (mainly French) is contrasted with the romantic drama of Shakespeare and Calderon, the poetry of perfection with the poetry of infinite desire.

(Wellek 1949: 6–7)

The classical–Romantic distinction, deriving at least in part from Schlegel, appeared publicly in England in lectures on literature given by Coleridge in 1812 and 1813 (Foakes 1987: I. 175). But these lectures were not published – and then only partially – until 1836–1839 when H. N. Coleridge published his four-volume edition of Coleridge's *Literary Remains*. The principal source of dissemination of Schlegel's ideas in Britain in the early nineteenth century was Madame de Stael's book *De L'Allemagne*, first published in French in London in 1813 and in English, also in London, almost at the same time. *De L'Allemagne* was reviewed favourably in Britain and familiarized some readers with German ideas on the classical and the Romantic. But despite such familiarity the idea of a contemporary specifically 'Romantic' group of writers in Britain does not at this stage seem to have taken deep hold in the British mind. Byron wrote to Goethe on 14 October 1820:

> I perceive that in Germany, as well as in Italy, there is a great struggle about what they call '*Classical*' and '*Romantic*' – terms which were not subjects of classification in England, at least when I left it four or five years ago. . . . Perhaps there may be something of the kind strung up lately, but I have not heard much about it, and it would be such bad taste that I shall be sorry to believe it.
>
> (Eichner 1972: 214)

Again, in 1831 Thomas Carlyle could declare that 'we are troubled with no controversies on Romanticism and classicism' (Eichner 1972: 214)

Certainly those writers that are now thought of as part of a Romantic movement in Britain never thought of themselves as such. The nearest that the early nineteenth century came to a substantial identification of a movement was Francis Jeffrey's attacks on what he termed the Lake School of poets, which included Wordsworth, Coleridge and Robert Southey. In a review of Southey's *Thalaba, the Destroyer* in the *Edinburgh Review* for October 1802 Jeffrey referred to a '*sect* of poets, that has established itself in this country within these ten or twelve years' (I. 63). He speaks of these poets as '*dissenters* from the established systems in poetry and criticism' and of their poetry as finding its source in the 'antisocial principles, and distempered sensibility of Rousseau – his discontent with the present constitution of society' (I. 63–64). Jeffrey's association of what he came to call the 'Lake Poets' with dissent had become by 1816 an association with the principle of revolution itself. In a review of Walter Scott's edition of the *Works of Jonathan Swift* in the *Edinburgh Review* for September 1816 Jeffrey observed, this time also finding German models for the 'Lake School', that:

> By far the most considerable change which has taken place in the world of letters, in our days, is that by which the wits of Queen Anne's [1665–1714] time have been gradually brought down from

the supremacy which they had enjoyed, without competition, for the best part of a century. When we were at our studies, some twenty-five years ago, we can perfectly remember that every young man was set to read Pope, Swift and Addison, as regularly as Virgil, Cicero and Horace. . . . All this, however, we take it, is now pretty well altered. . . . the revolution in our literature has been accelerated and confirmed by the concurrence of many causes. The agitations of the French Revolution . . . the impression of the new literature of Germany, evidently the original of our lake-school of poetry . . . the rise or revival of a general spirit of methodism in the lower orders – and the vast extent of our political and commercial relations . . . have brought knowledge and enterprise home.

(XXVII. 1, 8)

## POLITICS AND LITERATURE

Jeffrey's classification of 'Lake Poets', though it was taken up by contemporary commentators, was not a classification used of themselves by the poets in question. Yet it remains true that in the early nineteenth century there was a broad agreement that a significant shift – a revolution – in literary taste and values away from early eighteenth-century Neoclassicism had taken place. Commentators such as William Hazlitt drew – like Francis Jeffrey – a direct correlation between socio-political revolution and the literary 'revolution' in Britain. There was a precedent for making such a correlation in the 1800 Preface to *Lyrical Ballads*, where Wordsworth hinted at the idea of a necessary connection between 'society' and 'literature':

Several of my Friends are anxious for the success of these Poems . . . on this account they have advised me to prefix a systematic defence of the theory, upon which the poems were written. But I was unwilling to undertake the task. . . . For to treat the subject with the clearness and coherence, of which I believe it susceptible, it would be necessary to give a full account of the present state of the public taste in this country, and to determine how far this taste is healthy or depraved; which again could not be determined, without pointing out, in what manner language and the human mind act and react on each other, and without retracing the revolutions not of literature alone but likewise of society itself.

(Brett and Jones 1976: 242–43)

In his lecture 'On the Living Poets', published in 1818 in a volume entitled *Lectures on the English Poets*, William Hazlitt made an explicit connection between the Revolution in France and the new poetry in Britain. He was, as we shall see later, sceptical about how real this correspondence between socio-political and literary revolutions actually was. But for the moment we should note his elaboration of the kind of correspondence that had been suggested by Wordsworth:

Mr. Wordsworth is at the head of that which has been denominated the Lake school of poetry. . . . This school of poetry had its origin in the French revolution, or rather in those sentiments and opinions which produced that revolution; and which sentiments and opinions were indirectly imported into this country in translations from the German about that period. Our poetical literature had, towards the close of the last century, degenerated into the most trite, insipid, and mechanical of all things, in the hands of the followers of Pope and the Old French School of poetry. It wanted something to stir it up, and it found that something in the principles and events of the French revolution.

(Howe 1930–34: V. 161)

But the term 'Romantic', as a means of labelling this literary 'revolution' in Britain, was not in use in the early nineteenth century. The identification and historical description of a named British Romantic movement really began to take shape only in the second half of the century.

In literary histories from the mid century onwards there began to emerge a classification, more or less influenced by German ideas on the classical and the romantic, which can be seen as the precursor of more modern notions of British Romanticism. In 1864, for example, John Murray published *A History of English Literature*. This was a reprint, revised and enlarged by William Smith, of Thomas B. Shaw's *Outlines of English Literature*, published first in St Petersburg in 1846 and again in London in 1849. Chapter 19 of the 1864 book was entitled 'The Dawn of Romantic Poetry' and opens:

> The great revolution in popular taste and sentiment which substituted what is called the romantic type in literature for the cold and clear-cut artificial spirit of that classicism which is exhibited in its highest form in the writings of Pope was, like all powerful and durable movements, whether in politics or in letters, gradual. The mechanical perfection of the poetry of the age of Queen Anne had been imitated with such success that every versifier had caught the trick of melody and the neat antithetical opposition of thought; and indications soon began to be perceptible of a tendency to seek for subjects and forms of expressions in a wider, more passionate, and more natural sphere of nature and emotion.
>
> (Shaw 1864: 374)

The chapter goes on to survey 'pre-Romantic' eighteenth-century writers like Thomson, Beattie, Joseph and Thomas Warton, Akenside, Cowper, Macpherson, Chatterton and Burns, before the book leads into chapters on Thomas Percy and Walter Scott, on Byron, Thomas Moore, Shelley, Keats and Thomas Campbell, as well as on Southey, Coleridge and Wordsworth. The twentieth-century canon of Romantic writers is already established in all essentials.

By the 1880s and 1890s the term 'Romantic' had become relatively commonplace as a means of referring to writers of the late eighteenth and early nineteenth centuries who had reacted against early eighteenth-century Neoclassicism. In 1885 W. J. Courthope published a book entitled *The Liberal Movement in English Literature* – which concentrated on Wordsworth, Scott, Byron, Shelley, Coleridge and Keats – and of which Courthope said 'I might, indeed, have called the series "The Romantic Movement in English Literature"' (Courthope 1885: viii). As is apparent in the title that he decided upon, Courthope is interested in what he sees as the political associations of the literature he is dealing with. He reinscribes the correlation between socio-political revolution and Romanticism that had been noticed by early nineteenth-century commentators such as Jeffrey and Hazlitt. 'Let me say', he writes,

> that by the word 'literature' I mean imaginative literature, and especially poetry; and by 'Liberal Movement', the writings of those who, in point of time, followed the French Revolution, and who founded their matter and style on the principles to which that Revolution gave birth.
>
> (Courthope 1885: 22)

The connection between revolution and what was now called Romanticism was made again in 1897 by Edward Dowden in *The French Revolution and English Literature*:

> The closing years of the eighteenth century and the opening years of the nineteenth, with Burns and Blake, Coleridge and Keats, Byron and Shelley, are pre-eminent for the keenness and intensity of the lyrical cry in literature. A vast epic, however, of historical struggle, of national aspiration and national effort [the French Revolution], was being unrolled before the eyes of men. It did not stifle the lyrical cry of the Romantic poets, but it added a breadth and volume to their passions. . . . No one among his contemporaries was more deeply moved than

was Wordsworth by the great events in France. The character of his mind fitted him in a peculiar degree for receiving the full influence of the French Revolution.

(Dowden 1897: 158, 197)

Dowden's view characterizes what has been a major tendency in commentary on the Romantics from the early nineteenth century to the decades following the Second World War. He discerned a direct correlation between socio-political revolution and literary revolution, while at the same time establishing a special distinction between social revolution and aesthetic or spiritual change. For Dowden, Wordsworth was fitted 'for receiving the full influence of the French Revolution'. But it was the translation of that external revolutionary energy into internal, 'spiritual' terms that made Wordsworth a great poet. The actual politics of revolution were transmuted in Wordsworth into a discovery of 'the permanent politics of human nature' (Dowden 1897: 218). These 'permanent politics' were supposed to pertain to something essential in human nature which transcended particular historical events or conditions. But of course this view of Dowden's was itself political. Attending to purely inward qualities without reference to – or in distinction from – external social and political realities constituted an evasion of those realities. And this evasion amounted in effect to an endorsement of the social and political status quo of nineteenth-century England, however this endorsement was dressed up in quasi-mystical language concerning the 'nation's soul':

> Coleridge . . . has spoken of our greatest poet [Shakespeare] as embodying in his historical plays the permanent politics of human nature. It is a hard saying to understand or to expound. The permanent politics of human nature, – what are they? Of Wordsworth's 'Poems dedicated to National Independence and Liberty' we may assert that if they do not express such 'permanent politics', they have assuredly a purport passing beyond the occasions which suggested or inspired them. . . .

They deal not so much with events that pass away as with abiding forces of the heart of man and abiding truths of our corporate life. In external events he seeks an inward moral significance. . . . If we may speak of any single thought around which this remarkable group of poems is organized, it is this, – that the true life of a nation resides not in external institutions, not in visible prosperity, not in force of arms, not even in the splendours of individual genius, but in the spiritual energy of the people, in the vitality of that which animates all else, the nation's soul.

(Dowden 1897: 218–19)

Some writers in the early twentieth century refused Dowden's reading of Romanticism as the conversion of French revolutionary politics into an idea of purely spiritual transformation within a stable social and political order; they disagreed with his notion of Romanticism as the transmutation of radical political idealism into purely imaginative revolution and redemption. But they did not all laud the notion of politically revolutionary tendencies in Romanticism. In 1919, in *Rousseau and Romanticism*, the conservative Irving Babbitt saw such tendencies and expressly chose not to support Romanticism by speaking of its transubstantiation of external political force into internal imaginative or spiritual energy. Instead he identified Rousseau as the mainspring of Romanticism and – writing against the background of increasing democratization in the West and against the background of the 1917 Russian Revolution – he condemned what he saw as the utopian political collectivism of Romantic thought:

If we wish to see the psychology of Rousseau writ large we should turn to the French Revolution. . . . Rousseau and his disciple Robespierre were reformers in the modern sense, – that is they are concerned not with reforming themselves, but other men. Inasmuch as there is no conflict between good and evil in the breast of the beautiful soul he is free to devote all his efforts to the improvement of mankind, and he proposes to achieve this great end by diffusing the spirit of brotherhood. ... The world of Walt Whitman will be realized, a world in which there is neither inferior nor superior but only comrades. ... We need to keep in mind the special quality of Rousseau's sophistry if we wish to understand a very extraordinary circumstance during the past century. During this period men were moving steadily toward the naturalistic level, where the law of cunning and the law of force prevail, and at the same time had the illusion – or at least multitudes had the illusion – that they were moving towards peace and brotherhood. ... A liberty that means only emancipation from outer control will result ... in the most dangerous form of anarchy – anarchy of the imagination. On the degree of our perception of this fact will hinge the soundness of our use of another general term – democracy. We should beware above all of surrendering our imaginations to this word until it has been hedged about on every side with discriminations that have behind them all the experience of the past with this form of government.

(Babbitt 1919: 135–37, 373–74, 378)

By the 1930s and 1940s other writers were re-reading Romanticism not as something that laid the ground for the horrors of revolutionary collectivism but – in its stress on the non-rational and in its metaphysical absolutism – as something that prefigured Fascist totalitarianism. In a book published in 1942, for example, Albert Guerard was conscious of the threat posed to the world by German Nazi nationalism, a phenomenon which he saw as informed by a strain of Romanticism:

it is difficult to study either nineteenth century literature or nineteenth century history without being struck by the Romantic element in Nationalism. War, which is the ultimate test and the inevitable end of Nationalism, is, we must repeat, the failure of human reason; but the whole movement started

> by declaring the bankruptcy of human reason, by substituting the unconscious, the subconscious and the mystic for the rational. It is magnificent, but it is not sense. The Romantic rebellion against discipline, measure and sanity, that is to say against civilization, is the chief problem in European culture. . . . The ultimate development of Nationalism, Imperialism, is the most international of all diseases.
>
> That this delusion assumed in Germany a Romantic form is due to the moment when it became manifest, not any unique power or flaw in the German soul.
>
> (Guerard 1942: 43, 47–8)

Against this kind of association between Romanticism and Fascism Jacques Barzun had published in the *American Scholar* for 1941 an essay entitled 'To the Rescue of Romanticism'. Barzun was, in fact, one of the earliest of those commentators who, during and after the Second World War, sought to redefine Romanticism yet again – this time neither as communistic nor as fascistic but as a cultural phenomenon which could be seen to underpin the politics of western liberal democracy. In a book first published in 1943 Barzun rang the changes – in terms appropriate to the middle of the twentieth century – on the kind of reading of Romanticism that had been purveyed by Edward Dowden. That is to say, he stressed a connection between socio-political and literary revolution while at the same time purging Romanticism of any social and political associations which he found distasteful. Socio-political energies he converted into internal and spiritual ones, which were apparently somehow free of historical content:

> we need not be surprised that the romantic life was robust and productive, because, as we know, the romanticists were encouraged, stimulated, and justified by historical circumstances. The French Revolution and Napoleon had, in Stendhal's phrase, made a clean slate. But this stimulation was purely spiritual.
>
> (Barzun 1944: 117)

In a preface to the second edition of his book, first published in 1961, Barzun can be found making an argument which boils down to the idea that the 'spiritual' revolution of Romanticism was something that informs the politics of the contemporary western status quo – that is, the politics of the liberal democratic state:

> When originally published, my thesis had to meet the plausible arguments of those who believed that German and Italian fascism were Romanticism resurgent. Others thought that Russian communism was the logical consequence of Romantic socialism and nationalism. . . . But . . . the tendency of historic Romanticism was away from authority and toward liberty, away from the acceptance of caked wisdom and toward the exploratory development of the individual, away from the secure fixities and toward the drama of the unforseeable, away from monarchy and toward the sovereignty of the people. . . . Romanticism is populist (not to use the ambiguous word 'democratic') even when the Romanticist, like Scott or Carlyle, preaches a feudal order.
>
> (Barzun 1962: xx–xxi)

The attempt to define Romanticism in opposition to positions on the extreme left or, more particularly, on the extreme right was undertaken by other critics at this time. Northrop Frye's classic study of William Blake, *Fearful Symmetry*, first published in 1947 and written during the years of the Second World War, was, as Frye commented in a 1962 'Preface' to a reprint of the work, 'a book very much of its time'. It was, he said, 'haunted by Nazi Germany as a fulfilment of Blake's warnings about Druidism' (Frye 1962). Equally, an idea that the study of Romanticism has a positive value for citizens of the modern liberal democratic state echoes through M.H. Abrams' 1953 *The Mirror and the Lamp*. At the end of that book Abrams suggests that contemporary appreciation of Romantic poetry is a morally invigorating appreciation, something that can enhance the sense of individual freedom in contradistinction to totalizing socio-political forces. Romantic poetry, with its emphasis on individual feeling and imagination, is a worthy stimulus to 'a humanistic literary criticism' which carries an 'indictment of the brutalizing influence of an industrial and commercial society; and [an] insistence on individual values against the growing pressures toward mass conformity' (Abrams 1953: 334).

M.H. Abrams was arguably the most important single voice in the post-Second World War critical rehabilitation of Romanticism. This rehabilitation emanated largely, though not exclusively, from North America and was largely, though not exclusively, concerned with British Romanticism. In 1963 M.H. Abrams published an important and influential essay, 'English Romanticism: The Spirit of the Age', in a volume of four essays edited by Northrop Frye and entitled *Romanticism Reconsidered*.

Abrams' proposition in this piece is that Romantic poets 'were all centrally political and social poets' (Frye 1963: 43). For all of them the crucial political and social occurrence of recent times was, of course, the French Revolution. Abrams cites examples of the way a number of British people felt in the early years of the Revolution, from Wordsworth's wonderful retrospective pronouncement in *The Prelude*, 'Bliss was it in that dawn to be alive,/But to be young was very heaven!' (1805, x. 692–93; Wordsworth, Abrams and Gill 1979: 396), to the exuberant declaration of one of the leading men of the Whig party, Charles James Fox: 'How much the greatest event it is that ever happened in the world! and how much the best!' (Frye 1963: 31). What Abrams also notes is that the roots of specifically English radicalism lay with the religious Nonconformists of the seventeenth century. This meant that English radicals at the time of the French Revolution tended to interpret the Revolution in the light of the messianic, millennial, and apocalyptic framework of biblical prophecy. A renovated earth, a new Jerusalem, an era of virtue, justice, equality and peace was to be instituted through the Revolution. And poets declared themselves to be specially endowed with the capacity to envision this apocalypse. For example,

> The 'Introduction' to *Songs of Experience* (1794) calls on us to attend the voice which will sing all Blake's poems from now on: 'Hear the voice of the Bard!/Who Present, Past, & Future, sees', who calls to the lapsed Soul and enjoins the earth to cease her cycle and turn to the eternal day. This voice is that of the poet–prophets of the Old and New Testaments, now descending on Blake from its specifically British embodiment in that 'bard of old', John Milton. In his 'minor prophecies', ending in 1795, Blake develops, out of the heroic-scaled but still historical agents of his *French Revolution*, the Giant Forms of his later mythical system. The Bard becomes Los, the 'Eternal Prophet' and father of 'red Orc', who is the spirit of Energy bursting out in total spiritual, physical, and political revolution; the argument of the song sung by Los, however, remains that announced in *The French Revolution*.
>
> (Frye 1963: 40–41)

Blake's elevation of the function of the poet to the role of the visionary bard was, Abrams continues, a typically Romantic move and it was a move which, he says, has obscured for twentieth-century readers just how 'centrally political and social' the Romantic poets were:

> in many poems the Romantics do not write direct political and moral commentary but (in Schorer's apt phrase for Blake) 'the politics of vision', uttered in the persona of the inspired prophet–priest. ... Following the Miltonic example, the Romantic poet of the 1790s tried to incorporate what he regarded as the stupendous events of the age in the suitably great poetic forms. ... Whatever the form, the Romantic Bard is one 'who present, past, and future sees'; so that in dealing with current affairs his procedure is often panoramic, his stage

cosmic, his agents quasi-mythological, and his logic of events apocalyptic. Typically this mode of Romantic vision fuses history, politics, philosophy, and religion into one grand design, by asserting Providence – or some form of natural teleology – to operate in the seeming chaos of human history so as to effect from present evil a greater good; and through the mid-1790s the French Revolution functions as the symptom or early stage of the abrupt culmination of this design, from which will emerge a new man on a new earth which is a restored Paradise.

(Frye 1963: 44–46)

Abrams illustrates these points with references ranging from Robert Southey's *Joan of Arc: An Epic Poem*, written in 1793; to Coleridge's 'Religious Musings. A Desultory Poem, Written on Christmas' Eve, In the Year of Our Lord, 1794'; to Wordsworth's 'Descriptive Sketches', written in 1793; and even to Shelley's *Queen Mab*, written twenty or so years later:

In the first published version of [*Joan of Arc*] 1796, Book IX consists of a sustained vision of the realms of hell and purgatory, populated by the standard villains of the radicals' view of history. To Joan is revealed the Edenic past in the 'blest aera of the infant world', and man's fall, through lust for gold and power, to this 'theatre of woe'; yet 'for the best/Hath he ordained all things, the ALL-WISE' because man, 'Samson-like' shall 'burst his fetters' in a violent spasm not quite named the French Revolution. ... The year [in which 'Religious Musings' was written] is precisely that of Blake's *Europe: A Prophecy*, and like that poem, *Religious Musings* is clearly a revision for the time being of Milton's 'On the Morning of Christ's Nativity', which had taken the occasion of memorializing Christ's birth to anticipate 'The wakefull trump of doom' and the universal earthquake which will announce His Second Coming. . . . Wordsworth . . . concluded his . . . *Descriptive Sketches* with the prophecy . . . that the wars consequent on the French Revolution would fulfill the predictions . . . of the Book of Revelation. . . . Some two decades later Shelley recapitulated and expanded these poetic manifestations of the earlier 1790s. At the age of nineteen he began his first long poem, *Queen Mab*, in the mode of a vision of the woeful past, the ghastly present, and the blissful future, and . . . much of the imagery is imported from biblical millennialism.

(Frye 1963: 46–48, 50–51)

But Abrams is not primarily concerned with poems of the earlier 1790s. He is more interested in later Romantic works written after the failure of early revolutionary hope (this is, of course, to set aside the case of Shelley, who was born too late to have experienced the initial revolutionary fervour): 'The great Romantic poems were written not in the mood of revolutionary exaltation but in the later mood of revolutionary disillusionment or despair' (Frye 1963: 53). The idea that disillusionment with historical reality was the context within which the 'great' Romantic poems were written is the key to Abrams' understanding of what Romanticism was. He takes as his main example a passage from Wordsworth's *The Prelude*, which is a cardinal instance of a work composed after the collapse of early hopes for the actual renovation of humankind. Abrams refers to the sixth book of *The Prelude* where Wordsworth, having described his 1790 trip to revolutionary France and his intoxication with the sense of 'human nature seeming born again' (1805, VI. 354; Wordsworth, Abrams and Gill 1979: 204), goes on to describe his journey to the Simplon Pass:

On the Simplon road they had left their guide and climbed ever upward, until a peasant told them that they had missed their way and that the course now lay downwards.

> Loth to believe what we so grieved to hear,
> For still we had hopes that pointed to the clouds,
> We questioned him again, and yet again;

but every reply 'Ended in this, – *that we had crossed the Alps*'.

> Imagination . . .
> That awful Power rose from the mind's abyss
> Like an unfathered vapour that enraps,
> At once, some lonely traveller; I was lost;
> Halted without an effort to break through;
> But to my conscious soul I now can say –
> 'I recognise thy glory'.

Only now, in retrospect, does he recognise that his imagination had penetrated to the emblematic quality of the literal climb, in a revelation proleptic of the experience he was to recount in all the remainder of *The Prelude*. Man's infinite hopes can never be matched by the world as it is and man as he is, for these exhibit a discrepancy no less than that between his 'hopes that pointed to the clouds' and the finite height of the Alpine pass. But in the magnitude of the disappointment lies its consolation; for the flash of vision also reveals that infinite longings are inherent in the human spirit, and that the gap between the inordinacy of his hope and the limits of possibility is the measure of man's dignity and presence. ... In short, Wordsworth evokes from the unbounded and hence impossible hopes in the French Revolution a central Romantic doctrine; one which reverses the cardinal neoclassic ideal of setting only accessible goals, by converting what had been man's tragic error – the inordinacy of his 'pride' that persists in setting infinite aims for finite man – into his specific glory and his triumph . . . :

> Under such banners militant, the soul
> Seeks for no trophies, struggles for no spoils
> That may attest her prowess, blest in thoughts
> That are their own perfection and reward.

The militancy of overt political action has been transformed into the paradox of spiritual quietism: under such militant banners is no march, but a wise passiveness. This truth having been revealed to him, Wordsworth at once goes on to his apocalypse of nature in the Simplon Pass, where the *coincidentia oppositorum* of its physical attributes become the symbols of the biblical Book of Revelation:

> Characters of the great Apocalypse,
> The types and symbols of Eternity,
> Of first, and last, and midst, and without end.

(Frye 1963: 56–58)

Abrams goes on to point out that a similar conversion of millennial hope in literal revolution into a purely subjective hope is also the subject of Wordsworth's 'Prospectus' for the *The Recluse*, that grand three-part poem which was unfinished apart from *The Prelude* and *The Excursion* (1814). In 'The Prospectus' ('drafted as early as 1800'):

> the restoration of Paradise, as in the Book of Revelation, is . . . symbolized by a sacred marriage. But the hope has been shifted from the history of mankind to the mind of the single individual, from militant external action to an imaginative act; and the marriage between the Lamb and the New Jerusalem has been converted into a marriage between subject and object, mind and nature, which creates a new world out of the old world of sense:
>
> > For the discerning intellect of Man,
> > When wedded to this goodly universe
> > In love and holy passion, shall find these
> > A simple produce of the common day.
> > – I, long before the blissful hour arrives,
> > World chant, in lonely peace, the spousal verse

> Of this great consummation . . .
> And the creation (by no lower name
> Can it be called) which they with blended might
> Accomplish: – this is our high argument.

(Frye 1963: 59)

The practical consequences of Wordsworth's 'imaginative act' were not political but aesthetic. What Wordsworth did, in choosing the poor and outcast as subjects for much of his verse, was, says Abrams, to subvert 'a view of poetry inherited from the Renaissance':

> This view assumed and incorporated a hierarchical structure of social classes. In its strict form, it conceived poetry as an order of well-defined genres, controlled by a theory of decorum whereby the higher poetic kinds represent primarily kings and the aristocracy, the humbler classes . . . are relegated to the lowlier forms, and each poem is expressed in a level of style – high, middle, or low – appropriate, among other things, to the social status of its characters and the dignity of its genre. . . . Having given up the hope of revolutionizing the social and political structure, Wordsworth . . . discovered that his new calling, his divine 'mission' . . . is to effect through his poetry an egalitarian revolution of the spirit (what he elsewhere calls 'an entire regeneration' of his upper-class readers) so that they may share his revelation of the equivalence of souls, the heroic dimensions of common life, and the grandeur of the ordinary and the trivial in Nature.

(Frye 1963: 68–69)

What we have in Abrams' seminal essay is another version of Dowden's or Barzun's celebrations of Romanticism as something that makes a virtue out of the displacement of socio-political energy into internal or spiritual energy. Some years later Abrams greatly expanded his thesis – taking in a much wider range of

Romantic and later texts – in his book *Natural Supernaturalism. Tradition and Revolution in Romantic Literature* (1971). Here he summarizes his notion of Romanticism's assimilation of biblical and religious patterns of thought as follows:

> For Wordsworth and his contemporaries . . . the millennium didn't come. The millennial pattern of thinking, however, persisted, with this difference: the external means was replaced by an internal means for transforming the world. Such a substitution had a precedent early in the Christian era when, the assurance of an immediate Second Coming having been disappointed, Biblical exegetes postponed the literal millennium to an indefinite future. . . . Romantic literature, however, differs from these theological precedents in that its recourse is from one secular means of renovating the world to another. To put the matter with the sharpness of drastic simplification: faith in an apocalyse by revelation had been replaced by faith in an apocalypse by revolution, and this now gave way to faith in an apocalypse by imagination or cognition.
>
> (Abrams, 1971: 334)

The idea that Romanticism involved, above all else, an emphasis on the inner processes of the individual mind is an idea that was treated, in different ways, by a large number of commentators on Romanticism in the three decades or so following the Second World War. Two examples must suffice. My first is a 1963 essay, 'The Drunken Boat: The Revolutionary Element in Romanticism', in which Northrop Frye offered an account of what he took to be the essential revolutionary component of Romanticism. It was not, he wrote, a matter of ideas or of politics. It was 'primarily a revolution in poetic imagery': 'it may be possible for two poets to be related by common qualities of imagery even when they do not agree on a single thesis in religion, politics, or the theory of art itself' (Frye 1963: viii, 3). Frye starts by describing the framework which organizes the imagery of mediaeval and Renaissance poetry:

The most remarkable and obvious feature of this framework is the division of being into four levels. The highest level is heaven, the place of the presence of God. Next come the two levels of the order of nature, the human level and the physical level. The order of human nature, or man's proper home, is represented by the story of the Garden of Eden in the Bible and the myth of the Golden Age in Boethius and elsewhere. Man is no longer in it, but the end of all his religious, moral, and social cultivation is to raise him into something resembling it. Physical nature, the world of animals and plants, is the world man is now in, but unlike the animals and plants he is not adjusted to it. He is confronted from birth with a moral dialectic, and must either rise above it to his proper human home or sink below it into the fourth level of sin, death, and hell. This last level is not part of the order of nature, but its existence is what at present corrupts nature.

(Frye 1963: 3–4)

Of course, this kind of spatial projection of ideas of heaven and hell as well as of the human state in between, persisted well after the Renaissance. It is, indeed, still with us today, albeit in attenuated form or forms. But it exists side by side with another spatial ordering which, for Frye, was instituted at the time of Romanticism and was indeed the revolutionary element in Romanticism:

What I see first of all in Romanticism is the effect of a profound change, not primarily in belief, but in the spatial projection of reality. This in turn leads to a different localizing of the various levels of that reality. . . .

the metaphorical structure of Romantic poetry tends to move inside and downward instead of outside and upward, hence the creative world is deep within, and so is heaven or the place of the presence of God. Blake's Orc and Shelley's Prometheus are Titans imprisoned underneath experience; the Gardens of Adonis are down in [Keats'] *Endymion*, whereas they are up in

*The Faerie Queene* and [Milton's] *Comus*; in [Shelley's] *Prometheus Unbound* everything that aids mankind comes from below, associated with volcanoes and fountains. . . .

In pre-Romantic poetry heaven is the order of grace, and grace is normally thought of as descending from above into the soul. In the Romantic construct there is a center where inward and outward manifestations of a common motion and spirit are unified, where the ego is identified as itself because it is also identified with something which is not itself. In Blake this world at the deep center is Jerusalem, the City of God that mankind, or Albion, has sought all through history without success because he has been looking in the wrong direction, outside.

(Frye 1963: 5, 16–17)

Frye's is a powerful reading of the interiority of Romantic metaphoric structures. (Such structures can be seen to have entered the western imagination in a pervasive way. It would be possible, for example, to read the interior orientation of Sigmund Freud's psychoanalytic thought in the light of these structures.) But Northrop Frye's attempt to distinguish sharply the use of imagery from ideas or beliefs is not entirely persuasive. And in the end his essay represents a variation on the kind of attempt made by M.H. Abrams to speak of revolution in the context of Romanticism as a purely internal or spiritual principle. In Frye's account of Romantic imagery there is a tendency to examine the deployment of that imagery as a formal issue which can be considered without reference to the social, political and intellectual context within which the form was generated.

Another comparable variant is to be found in the writing of Harold Bloom. In 1969 Bloom published in *The Yale Review* an essay, 'The Internalization of Quest-Romance', in which he considered the inwardness of the British Romantics in terms of the genre of quest-romance. The essay was republished in 1970 in a landmark collection of essays edited by Bloom himself and entitled *Romanticism and Consciousness. Essays in Criticism*:

> English Romanticism legitimately can be called, as traditionally it has been, a revival of romance. More than a revival, it is an internalization of romance, particularly of the quest variety, an internalization made for more than therapeutic purposes, because made in the humanizing hope that approaches apocalyptic intensity. The poet takes the patterns of quest-romance and transposes them into his own imaginative life. . . .
>
> The movement of quest-romance, before its internalization by the High Romantics, was from nature to redeemed nature, the sanction of redemption being the gift of some external spiritual authority, sometimes magical. The Romantic movement is from nature to the imagination's freedom . . . and the imagination's freedom is frequently purgatorial, redemptive in direction but destructive of the social self.
>
> (Bloom 1970: 5–6)

Bloom, like Abrams, adopts the term 'revolutionary' not in a socio-political but in a subjectivist dimension:

> Frye, in his theory of myths, explores the analogue between quest-romance and the dream: 'Translated into dream terms, the quest-romance is the search of the libido or desiring self for a fulfilment that will deliver it from the anxieties of reality but will still contain that reality'. Internalized romance – and *The Prelude* and *Jerusalem* can be taken as the greatest examples of this kind – traces a Promethean and revolutionary quest, and cannot be translated into dream terms, for in it the libido turns inward into the self. . . . The hero of internalized quest is the poet himself, the antagonists of quest are everything in the self that blocks imaginative work, and the fulfilment is never the poem itself, but the poem beyond that is made possible by the apocalypse of imagination. . . . In Romantic quest the

Promethean hero stands finally, quite alone, upon a tower that
is only himself, and his stance is all the fire there is. . . .

The dangers of idealizing the libido are of course constant in
the life of the individual, and such idealizations are dreadful for
whole societies, but the internalization of quest-romance had
to accept these dangers.

(Bloom 1970: 8–9)

The problem with Bloom's suggestive account of Romantic
internalized quest is that while he touches on the dangers of
such internalization for 'whole societies', he proceeds nevertheless to accept Romanticism on its own terms and to celebrate the
internalizing enterprise as a 'humanizing' one, without questioning
whether humane values can be arrived at in isolation or in
distinction from social reality.

However, before I move into socially and historically minded
criticism of the view of Romanticism held by critics such as
Abrams, Frye or Bloom, I want to summarize another kind of
negative criticism of the Abrams line of thought which came in
the 1970s and 1980s from deconstructionist and associated poststructuralist commentators.

## POSTSTRUCTURALISM AND ROMANTICISM

Here I must recount, first, the ideas of Romantic symbolism held
by Abrams and others. In his essay 'English Romanticism: The
Spirit of the Age', Abrams spoke of the way in which Romantic
hope is centred on 'the mind of the single individual' and of the
way in which a traditional religious hope for 'the restoration of
Paradise . . . symbolized by a sacred marriage' is converted in
Romanticism into the ideal of 'a marriage between subject and
object, mind and nature, which creates a new world out of the old
world of sense' (quoted p. 99). For Abrams the dialectic between
subject and object, between mind and nature, and the hope of
synthesizing the two terms of the dialectic lie at the heart of

Romanticism. And equally at the heart of Romanticism is the view that it is the purpose of art, and specifically of the symbolic in art, to effect this synthesis. In a 1965 essay, 'Structure and Style in the Greater Romantic Lyric', Abrams invoked Coleridge to support this view. For Coleridge, Abrams writes, what was wrong in the older philosophical traditions of both Descartes and Locke was their insistence on the complete separation between mind and matter, 'which replaced a providential, vital, and companionable world by a world of particles in purposeless movement' (Bloom 1970: 217). Equally wrong in those two traditions 'was the method of reasoning underlying this dualism, that pervasive elementarism which takes as its starting point the irreducible element or part and conceives all wholes to be a combination of discrete parts, whether material atoms or mental "ideas"' (Bloom 1970: 217). For Coleridge, this kind of elementarism led to a vision of a universe that lacked any informing spirit, any vital principle of unity. The universe was an aggregate of dead parts, a universe of death. In *The Excursion*, Wordsworth's Wanderer, seeking to correct the despondency of the Solitary, also expressed the view that an atomized universe is a sterile one:

> Enquire of ancient Wisdom; go, demand
> Of mighty Nature, if 'twas ever meant
> That we should pry far off yet be unraised;
> That we should pore, and dwindle as we pore,
> Viewing all objects unremittingly
> In disconnexion dead and spiritless;
> And still dividing, and dividing still,
> Break down all grandeur.
>
> (IV. 957–64; de Selincourt 1972: 139)

Coleridge put his view of the matter in *The Friend* (1809–1810):

> The ground-work . . . of all true philosophy is the full apprehen-
> sion of the difference between . . . that intuition of things which

> arises when we possess ourselves, as one with the whole . . . and
> that which presents itself when . . . we think of ourselves as
> separated beings, and place nature in antithesis to the mind,
> as object to subject, thing to thought, death to life.
>
> (Bloom 1970: 218)

'To the Romantic sensibility', says Abrams, a universe reduced by analysis into an inert collection of parts, in which everything, including the human subject, is alienated from every other thing,

> could not be endured, and the central enterprise common to
> many post-Kantian German philosophers and poets, as well as
> to Coleridge and Wordsworth, was to join together the 'subject'
> and 'object' that modern intellection had put asunder, and thus
> to revivify a dead nature, restore its concreteness, significance,
> and human values, and re-domiciliate man in a world which
> had become alien to him.
>
> (Bloom 1970: 218)

Abrams notes Coleridge's emphases in the *Biographia Literaria* on the 'primary IMAGINATION' as a 'repetition in the finite mind of the eternal act of creation in the infinite I AM' and on the 'secondary Imagination', whose visions are embodied in artistic creation, as partaking in the nature of the 'primary IMAGINATION'. Artistic creativity is understood by Coleridge to share in the nature of divine creativity: the spirit of such creativity being to synthesize and unify, to reconcile disparateness and to overcome discord. Abrams observes that

> In the *Biographia Literaria*, when Coleridge came to lay down his
> own metaphysical system, he based it on a premise designed
> to overcome both the elementarism in method and the dualism
> in theory of knowledge of his eighteenth-century predecessors,
> by converting their absolute division between subject and object
> into a logical 'antithesis', in order to make it eligible for resolu-
> tion by the Romantic dialectic of thesis–antithesis–synthesis.

The 'primary ground' of his theory of knowledge, he says, is 'the coincidence of an object with a subject' or 'of the thought with the thing', in a synthesis, or 'coalescence', in which the elements lose their separate identities. 'In the reconciling, and recurrence of this contradiction exists the process and mystery of production and life'. And the process of vital artistic creation reflects the process of this vital creative perception. Unlike the fancy, which can only rearrange the 'fixities and definites' of sense-perception without altering their identity, the 'synthetic and magical power' of the secondary imagination repeats the primal act of knowing by dissolving the elements of perception 'in order to recreate' them, and 'reveals itself in the balance or reconciliation of opposite or discordant qualities' – including the reconciliation of intellect with emotion, and of thought with object: 'the idea, with the image'.

(Bloom 1970: 219–20)

Coleridge's idea, expressed in chapter 14 of *Biographia Literaria*, that the poet possesses a power of 'imagination' which 'reveals itself in the balance or reconciliation of opposite or discordant qualities: of . . . the idea, with the image' (Shawcross 1907: II.12) moves Abrams to contrast the allegorical modes of pre-Romantic writing with the symbolic modes of Romantic writing. In pre-Romantic poetry dealing with landscape the objects of nature are described and a reflection or a moral is, as it were, simply appended to the description of the natural object. The '*paysage moralisé* was not', says Abrams,

invented as a rhetorical device by poets, but was grounded on two collateral and pervasive concepts in mediaeval and Renaissance philosophy. One of these was the doctrine that God has supplemented the Holy Scriptures with the *liber creaturarum*, so that objects of nature . . . show forth the attributes and providence of their Author. The second concept, of independent philosophic origin but often fused with the first, is that the divine

Architect has designed the universe analogically, relating the physical, moral, and spiritual realms by an elaborate system of correspondences. A landscape, accordingly, consists of *verba visibilia*. . . .

Thus Henry Vaughan, musing over a waterfall, was enabled by the guidance of its Creator to discover its built-in correspondences with the life and destiny of man:

> What sublime truths and wholesome themes,
> Lodge in thy mystical deep streams!
> Such as dull man can never find
> Unless that spirit lead his mind
> Which first upon thy face did move,
> And hatched all with his quick'ning love.

In 1655, the year in which Vaughan published 'The Waterfall', Denham added to his enlarged edition of 'Cooper's Hill' the famous pair of couplets on the Thames which link description to concepts by a sustained parallel between the flow of the stream and the ideal conduct of life and art:

> O could I flow like thee, and make thy stream
> My great example, as it is my theme!
> Though deep, yet clear, though gentle, yet not dull,
> Strong without rage, without o'erflowing, full.

> (Bloom 1970: 209)

Denham's *Cooper's Hill* provided a model for eighteenth-century locodescriptive poetry, a poetry which continued in a broadly allegorical mode; a mode where a literal level of signification, a description of an object in a landscape, co-exists with an idea or concept that is taken to be signified by the literal object. In allegory, as understood by, say, Coleridge or Abrams, there always remain two levels: the described object, the image, on the one hand, and a concept that is signified by and runs parallel to that image on the other. Coleridge contrasted allegory with symbol, suggesting that in the case of the symbol it is not possible to make a separation between image (or 'picture-language', below) and idea (or 'abstract notion', below). In the case of the symbol there is only the image which itself shares in the nature of that which it is taken to represent, as Coleridge declares in *The Statesman's Manual* (1816):

> Now an Allegory is but a translation of abstract notions into a picture-language which is itself nothing but an abstraction from objects of the senses; the principal being more worthless even than its phantom proxy, both alike unsubstantial, and the former shapeless to boot. On the other hand a Symbol . . . is characterized by a translucence of the Special [the species] in the Individual or of the General [the genus] in the Especial or of the Universal in the General. Above all by the translucence of the Eternal through and in the Temporal. It always partakes of the Reality which it renders intelligible; and while it enunciates the whole, abides itself as a living part in that Unity of which it is the representative. The other [allegories] are but empty echoes which the fancy arbitrarily associates with apparitions of matter.
>
> (White 1972: 30)

Accordingly, for Coleridge, who was interested above all else in reconciling difference, the symbolic mode is superior to the allegorical. Abrams speaks of Coleridge's 'Dejection: An Ode' as the type of the Romantic symbolic mode:

> 'Dejection: An Ode' . . . is a triumph of the 'coadunating' imagination, in the very poem which laments the severance of his community with nature and the suspension of his shaping spirit of imagination. In unspoken consonance with the change of the outer scene and of the responsive wind-harp from ominous quiet to violent storm to momentary calm, the poet's

mind, momentarily revitalized by a correspondent inner breeze, moves from torpor through violence to calm, by a process in which the properties earlier specified of the landscape – the spring rebirth, the radiated light of moon and stars, the clouds and rain, the voice of the harp – reappear as the metaphors of the evolving meditation on the relation of mind to nature. . . . On Coleridge's philosophical premises, in this poem nature is made thought and thought nature, both by their sustained interaction and by their seamless metaphoric continuity.

The best Romantic meditations on a landscape, following Coleridge's examples, all manifest a transaction between subject and object in which the thought incorporates and makes explicit what was already implicit in the outer scene. . . . When the Romantic poet confronted a landscape, the distinction between self and not-self tended to dissolve.

(Bloom 1970: 223)

The idea that an analogical principle practically disappears in Romantic poetry ('nature is made thought and thought nature') is something that can be found directing the work of other commentators on Romanticism in the post-Second World War years. To take one example: in 1954, ten years or so before Abrams produced his piece on the 'Greater Romantic Lyric', W.K. Wimsatt published an essay entitled 'The Structure of Romantic Nature Imagery'. In this essay Wimsatt compared a 1789 sonnet by William Lisle Bowles, 'To the River Itchin', with Coleridge's 1796 'To the River Otter'. The subject of the Bowles sonnet is the reflections of its speaker on times when, as a boy, he was happy beside the banks of the river. Age has brought disappointment and loss of friends, and returning to think of past happiness by the river brings both sadness and consolation. But the imaginative structure of the sonnet, says Wimsatt, is different from what was to pertain in Romantic poems. Two different things, the literal river and the speaker's thoughts about the river, are linked but remain distinct:

'the total impression is one of simple association (by contiguity in time) simply asserted' (Bloom 1970: 80). By contrast, Wimsatt declares that in Coleridge's poem, which in paraphrase would be similar to Bowles', the object described or image and the idea are not merely associated, they are fused at source:

> there is a rich ground of meaning in Coleridge's sonnet beyond what is overtly stated. The descriptive details of his sonnet gleam brightly because . . . he has invested them with significance. . . . The metaphor in fact is scarcely noticed by the main statement of the poem. Both tenor and vehicle, furthermore, are wrought in a parallel process out of the same material. The river landscape is both the occasion of reminiscence and the source of the metaphors by which reminiscence is described. . . . To return to our metaphysics – of an inanimate, plastic Nature, not transcending but immanent in and breathing through all things – and to discount for the moment such differences as may relate to Wordsworth's naturalism, Coleridge's theology, Shelley's Platonism, or Blake's visions: we may observe that the common feat of the romantic nature poets was to read meanings into the landscape. The meaning might be such as we have seen in Coleridge's sonnet, but it might more characteristically be more profound, concerning the spirit or soul of things – 'the one life within us and abroad'. And that meaning especially was summoned out of the very surface of nature itself. It was embodied imaginatively and without the explicit religious or philosophic statements which one will find in classical or Christian instances.
>
> (Bloom 1970: 82–83)

The view that Romanticism set itself the task of overcoming the split between subject and object, and the celebration of Romantic poetry as something that, in its symbolic procedures, indeed resolved this difference and succeeded in representing the 'one Life, within us and abroad', were perspectives that were called into question by the critic Paul de Man. De Man practised an early type of deconstruction – an undermining of the very foundations of systems of thought – in an essay which first appeared in 1969, 'The Rhetoric of Temporality'. De Man sets about challenging in this essay the view that values symbol more highly than allegory. He surveys the history of rhetorical figures from the later eighteenth through the nineteenth centuries, when the term 'symbol' tended to replace other terms for figural language, including 'allegory', and cites a 1960 study by Hans-Georg Gadamer, *Wahrheit und Methode*, in which Gadamer sees 'the valorization of symbol at the expense of allegory' coinciding

> with the growth of an aesthetics that refuses to distinguish between experience and the representation of this experience. ... Allegory appears as dryly rational and dogmatic in its reference to a meaning that it does not itself constitute, whereas the symbol is founded on an intimate unity between the image that rises up before the senses and the supersensory totality that the image suggests.
>
> (de Man 1983: 188–89)

But, says de Man, such aesthetics are founded on false premises. He shows how it is possible to read Coleridge's preference for symbol over allegory (argued in *The Statesman's Manual*, quoted above, p. 110) in a way in which the claimed distinction between symbol and allegory actually begins to disappear:

> in the passage from *The Statesman's Manual* ... a certain degree of ambiguity is manifest. After associating the essential thinness of allegory with a lack of substantiality, Coleridge wants to stress, by contrast, the worth of the symbol. One would expect the latter to be valued for its organic or material richness, but instead the notion of 'translucence' is suddenly put in evidence. ...
>
> The material substantiality dissolves and becomes a mere

reflection of a more original unity that does not exist in the material world.

(de Man 1983: 192)

Despite this idea of the symbol as a reflection of a unity that is higher than the material world, Coleridge goes on, de Man points out, to condemn allegory for *its* status as a reflection:

It is all the more surprising to see Coleridge . . . characterize allegory negatively as being *merely* a reflection. In truth, the spiritualization of the symbol has been carried so far that the moment of material existence by which it was originally defined has now become altogether unimportant; symbol and allegory alike now have a common origin beyond the world of matter. . . . Both figures designate, in fact, the transcendental source, albeit in an oblique and ambiguous way. Coleridge stresses the ambiguity in a definition of allegory in which it is said that allegory ' . . . convey[s], while in disguise, either moral qualities or conceptions of the mind that are not in themselves objects of the senses . . . ', but then goes on to state that, on the level of language, allegory can 'combine the parts to form a consistent whole'. Starting out from the assumed superiority of the symbol in terms of organic substantiality, we end up with a description of figural language as translucence, a description in which the distinction between allegory and symbol has become of secondary importance.

(de Man 1983: 192–93)

Yet while the distinction may, when Coleridge is read in this way, be of secondary importance, the influence of Coleridge on post-Second World War criticism has been in the direction of endorsing the idea of the superiority of the symbolic over the allegoric. In such criticism, de Man writes,

the conception of metaphor that is being assumed, often with explicit reference to Coleridge, is that of a dialectic between object and subject, in which the experience of the object takes on the form of a perception or a sensation. The ultimate intent of the image is not, however, as in Coleridge, translucence, but synthesis, and the mode of this synthesis is defined as 'symbolic' by the priority conferred on the initial moment of sensory perception. . . . Abrams makes it seem, at times [in 'Structure and Style in the Greater Romantic Lyric'], as if the Romantic theory of imagination did away with analogy altogether and that Coleridge in particular replaced it by a genuine and working monism. 'Nature is made thought and thought nature', he writes, 'both by their sustained interaction and by their seamless metaphoric continuity'. But he does not really claim that this degree of fusion is achieved and sustained – at most that it corresponds to Coleridge's desire for a unity toward which his thought and poetic strategy strive. Analogy as such is certainly never abandoned as an epistemological pattern for natural images. . . . Nevertheless, the relationship between mind and nature becomes indeed a lot less formal, less purely associative and external than it is in the eighteenth century.

(de Man 1983: 193, 195)

And to express this less purely associative relationship criticism has, says de Man, resorted to words less formal than analogy; words such as 'affinity' or 'sympathy':

the new terminology indicates a gliding away from the formal problem of a congruence between the two poles to that of the ontological priority of the one over the other. For terms such as 'affinity' or 'sympathy' apply to the relationships between subjects rather than to relationships between a subject and an object. The relationship with nature has been superseded by an inter-subjective, interpersonal relationship that, in the last analysis, is a relationship of the subject toward itself. Thus the priority has passed from the outside world entirely within the subject, and we end up with something that resembles a radical idealism.

(de Man 1983: 195–96)

But the view that Romanticism is just such an idealism, that it simply asserts the priority of the subject over objective nature, meets problems when it comes to Romantic poetry that appears to assert the substantial reality of nature in distinction from the observing consciousness. The confusion or contradiction is to be found, de Man suggests, within Romantic poetry itself as well as in criticism that simply repeats the contradiction:

> Wordsworth . . . sees the . . . dialectic between the self and nature in temporal terms. The movements of nature are for him instances of . . . endurance within a pattern of change, the assertion of a metatemporal, stationary state beyond the apparent decay of a mutability that attacks certain outward aspects of nature but leaves the core intact. Hence we have famous passages such as the description of the mountain scenes in *The Prelude* in which a striking temporal paradox is evoked:

> These forests unapproachable by death,
> That shall endure as long as man endures . . .
> The immeasurable height
> Of woods decaying, never to be decayed
> The stationary blast of waterfalls.

> Such paradoxical assertions of eternity in motion can be applied to nature but not to a self caught up entirely within mutability. The temptation exists, then, for the self to borrow, so to speak, the temporal stability that it lacks from nature, and to devise strategies by means of which nature is brought down to a human level while still escaping from 'the unimaginable touch of time.' This strategy is certainly present in Coleridge. And it is present, though perhaps not consciously, in critics such as Abrams and Wasserman, who see Coleridge as the great synthesizer and who take his dialectic of subject and object to be the authentic pattern of romantic imagery. But this

forces them, in fact, into a persistent contradiction. They are obliged, on the one hand, to assert the priority of object over subject that is implicit in an organic conception of language. So Abrams states: 'The best Romantic meditations on a landscape, following Coleridge's example, all manifest a transaction between subject and object in which the thought incorporates and makes explicit what was already implicit in the outer scene.' This puts the priority unquestionably in the natural world, limiting the task of the mind to interpreting what is given in nature. Yet this statement is taken from the same paragraph in which Abrams quotes the passages from Wordsworth and Coleridge that confer an equally absolute priority to the self over nature. The contradiction reaches a genuine impasse.

(de Man 1983: 196–98)

De Man goes on to cite Abrams' statement, in his essay on the 'Greater Romantic Lyric', that the difference between the Romantic lyric and seventeenth-century meditations on nature turns on the representation of place. In the seventeenth century, the '"composition of place" was not a specific locality . . . but was a typical scene or object, usually called up . . . before "the eyes of the imagination", in order to set off and guide the thought by means of correspondences whose interpretation was firmly controlled by an inherited typology' (Bloom 1970: 228). In Romantic poetry, however, the *actual* geographical place becomes of paramount importance and the meanings 'educed from the scene are not governed by a public symbolism, but have been brought to it by the private mind which perceives it' (Bloom 1970: 228). But, de Man argues, the Romantic representation of geographical place is not always as concrete and specific as Abrams suggests:

in observing the development of even as geographically concrete a poet as Wordsworth, the significance of the locale can extend so far as to include a meaning that is no longer circumscribed by the literal horizon of a given place. The meaning of the site is often made problematic by a sequence of spatial ambiguities, to such an extent that one ends up no longer at a specific place but with a mere name whose geographical significance has become almost meaningless. . . . Passages in Wordsworth such as the crossing of the Alps or the ascent of Mount Snowden [sic] . . . can no longer be classified with the locodescriptive poem of the eighteenth century. In the terminology proposed by Abrams, passages of this kind no longer depend on the choice of a specific locale, but are controlled by 'a traditional and inherited typology', exactly as in the case of the poems from the sixteenth and seventeenth centuries – with this distinction, however, that the typology is no longer the same.

(de Man 1983: 203)

In other words, the apocalyptic associations involved in, say, Wordsworth's presentation of his crossing of the Alps in Book VI of *The Prelude*, associations which Abrams himself links with the Book of Revelation (see p. 99), are themselves part of a traditional and inherited conceptual system. Rather than working the tenor and the vehicle of his metaphor out of the same material, Wordsworth is grafting on to his account of the Simplon Pass a significance derived from an ancient European thought-system. Wordsworth's poetry of place is in this instance less symbolic in the Coleridgean sense than allegoric, in that two terms, the literal description and the significance of that description, are distinguishable. De Man speaks of Wordsworth's 'allegorization of the geographical site' and says that 'the prevalence of allegory always corresponds to the unveiling of an authentically temporal destiny. This unveiling takes place in a subject that has sought refuge against the impact of time in a natural world to which, in truth, it bears no resemblance':

In the world of the symbol it would be possible for the image to coincide with the substance, since the substance and its representation do not differ in their being but only in their extension: they are part and whole of the same set of categories. Their relationship is one of simultaneity, which, in truth, is spatial in kind, and in which the intervention of time is merely a matter of contingency, whereas, in the world of allegory, time is the originary constitutive category. The relationship between the allegorical sign and its meaning (*signifie*) is not decreed by dogma. . . . We have, instead, a relationship between signs in which the reference to their respective meanings has become of secondary importance. But this relationship between signs necessarily contains a constitutive temporal element; it remains necessary, if there is to be allegory, that the allegorical sign refer to another sign that precedes it. The meaning constituted by the allegorical sign can then consist only in the *repetition* (in the Kierkegaardian sense of the term) of a previous sign with which it can never coincide, since it is of the essence of this previous sign to be pure anteriority.

(de Man 1983: 207)

A little later de Man declares that through its constitution in time allegory 'prevents the self from an illusory identification with the non-self'. The persistence of allegory in Romantic poetry, de Man argues, constitutes an implicit acknowledgement of something which is repressed in the Romantics' own more theoretical statements: the essential temporality or finiteness of the self and of the language used by the self which, just because they are finite, can never achieve an identity with absolute or transcendent truth. De Man is happy to have found a way of showing that, for all their eulogy of the symbolic, the Romantics may be discovered working still in an allegorical mode, since the crucial thing about allegory is that it is not as 'mystified' about its own status as a figurative or rhetorical device; as, in other words, a construction or fiction.

Whereas the symbol postulates the possibility of an identity or identification, allegory designates primarily a distance in relation to its own origin, and, renouncing the nostalgia and the desire to coincide, it establishes its language in the void of this temporal difference. In so doing, it prevents the self from an illusory identification with the non-self, which is now fully, though painfully, recognized as a non-self. It is this painful knowledge that we perceive at the moments when early romantic literature finds its true voice. It is ironically revealing that this voice is so rarely recognized for what it really is and that the literary movement in which it appears has repeatedly been called a primitive naturalism or a mystified solipsism. The authors with whom we are dealing had often gone out of their way to designate their theological and philosophical sources. ...

We are led, in conclusion, to a historical scheme that differs entirely from the customary picture. The dialectical relationship between subject and object is no longer the central statement of romantic thought, but this dialectic is now located entirely in the temporal relationships that exist within a system of allegorical signs. It becomes a conflict between a conception of the self seen in its authentically temporal predicament and a defensive strategy that tries to hide from this negative self-knowledge. On the level of language the asserted superiority of the symbol over allegory, so frequent during the nineteenth century, is one of the forms taken by this tenacious self-mystification.

(de Man 1983: 207–208)

Nor is it possible to find a language – itself a temporal and finite phenomenon – which can share in the nature of a reality that is beyond time and space. The two, self and language, are of course mutually implicated in poststructuralist thought. It is not that the self exists separate from language and simply uses it to express itself. The self, in the sense of the fully self-conscious human adult, does not exist outside of language and other sign-systems. In order to represent itself to itself, in order to be a self-conscious creature, in order simply to be, the self must use signs, verbal or otherwise. And, again, it does not merely 'use' signs as if it were detachable from them; it is, rather, coincident with them, it is constituted out of them. No self escapes the bounds of language and sign-systems and no language or other sign-system escapes temporality. Romanticism's claims to have found through symbolic language a means of uniting the subject, the self, in all its temporality, with a larger, often transcendental, object were a delusion. They were a delusion occasionally recognized or half-recognized in Romantic poetry itself; in Shelley's 'Alastor', for instance, which explores the potential futility of any projected dissolution of the gap between self and ideal other; a perception that the Romantic celebration of an ideal subjectivity may be nothing more than glamourization of solipsistic vacancy. Catherine Belsey has summarized a post-structuralist perspective on the self-cancelling logic of Romantic dreams of reconciling subject and the object in a way which gives priority to the subject. If Romanticism set itself the task of envisioning a dissolution of boundaries between subject and object, it is

> the heroic impossibility of this task which produces Romantic exultation and despair. The obliteration of the object in a subjectivity which expands to incorporate it ('in our life alone does nature live' [Coleridge, 'Dejection: An Ode', l. 48]) is the negation of desire, because desire depends on the existence of an object that can be desired precisely in so far as it is outside the subject, radically other. The negation of desire, imaginary plenitude, presents a world whose existence and meaning depends on the presence of the subject, a world of absolute subjectivity. But the obliteration of the object implies the fading of the subject, because it is also the negation of difference.
>
> (Belsey 1986: 68–69)

Allegory, for de Man, is preferable to the mystifications of the symbolic because it acknowledges its own temporal and finite nature. It does not claim to be able to effect a union between a temporally defined and bound subjectivity and a realm outside of time. To have called in question the priority of the symbolic over the allegoric in Romantic poetry was to have raised questions about the entire interpretive frame of reference used by critics of the Abrams tendency of mind in their reading of Romanticism. And in raising such questions de Man opened the way for deconstructive and associated readings of Romantic verse.

In the wake of de Man's essay numerous critics in the 1970s and 1980s began to interpret the basic strategy of Romantic poetry as one in which the poets sought to evade recognition simultaneously of their own temporality and the temporality of the language within which the self is constituted. In 1984 Arden Reed collected a number of essays on Romanticism, several dating from the late 1970s, which were influenced by poststructuralist ideas. The collection was called *Romanticism and Language*, a title which recalled Harold Bloom's 1970 collection *Romanticism and Consciousness*. The new title marked the way in which a significant section of critical interest was no longer focused on consciousness as some kind of pure entity, but on consciousness as something that cannot be considered separately from language. Timothy Bahti provided an essay on Wordsworth's poetry, 'Wordsworth's Rhetorical Theft', in which he explicitly refused to 'presuppose a *self* whose consciousness would then be found in some relation to figural language'; rather, he assumed that 'structures of language' are 'the condition of possibility . . . for the self and its faculties of consciousness'(Reed 1984: 99). Mary Jacobus provided an essay on Romantic autobiography, 'The Art of Managing Books: Romantic Prose and the Writing of the Past', in which she concentrated on views of language advanced by Thomas de Quincey, William Hazlitt and Charles Lamb. She framed her discussion of these three prose writers of the Romantic period with a commentary on the antagonism which Wordsworth displayed in Book V of *The Prelude* towards the imposition of bookish learning on children's minds:

Book learning . . . gets short shrift from an educational point of view, and the whole drift of Book V is toward subsuming literature under the heading of Nature – toward naturalizing it as 'only less,/For what we may become . . . Than Nature's self'.

Wordsworth's. . . . attack on regimentation and conditioning – rote learning designed to turn children into 'engines' – discloses the unease that underlies much Romantic writing about literacy. . . . The fear covertly expressed in Book V is that it is not we that write, but writing that writes us; that the writing of the past, rather than 'the spirit of the past' (XI, 342), determines 'what we may become'; and that the language of books is 'unremittingly and noiselessly at work' (in Wordsworth's memorably obsessed phrases) to derange and to subvert the language of incarnated thought on which Romantic theorists pin their hope of linguistic salvation.

(Reed 1984: 216)

For Jacobus, Wordsworth's endeavour throughout *The Prelude* is to avoid a realization that the self is constituted by language and that linguistic signs do not refer transparently to a reality outside themselves; they take their meaning, rather, only in relation to other signs. A word gains its meaning in a system of differences from other words, not because it has an intrinsic or essential connection with anything beyond itself. Such a realization is evaded by Wordsworth because it would empty the self of the substance and transcendental dimension that he would attribute to it. In her essay Jacobus distils from the work of prose writers of the Romantic period greater recognition of the emptiness of language and hence of the self than is apparent in Wordsworth's poetry:

Casting about for an epic subject at the start of *The Prelude*, Wordsworth recoils disheartened from the histories of Britain, myth, Liberty, heroism, or the everyday left unsung by previous epic poets; recoils, in effect, from the history of past writing and from the writing of the past:

> The whole Fabric seems to lack
> Foundation, and, withal, appears throughout
> Shadowy and unsubstantial.

> It is not so much the burden of the past that inhibits him as this glimpse of the insubstantiality inherent in all writing – in autobiography as well as epic. The remaining thirteen books of *The Prelude* are an attempt to clothe transparency and provide foundations for fabric that cannot be gainsaid, the history of his own mind. Romantic prose writers remind us what 'The Growth of a Poet's Mind' owes to the art of managing books; they tell the one story Wordsworth could not afford to tell at any price – that the language of books can only be the history of itself.
>
> (Reed 1984: 246)

Poststructuralist readings of British Romantic writing have often been penetrating and illuminating, exposing unselfconscious or unstated contradictions, illogicalities and evasions in the very fabric of the writing. It is sometimes possible to feel, however, that the approach is reductively formalist in the sense that it could be applied to almost any literary text of any period and the same conclusions, in principle, could be drawn. The only kind of literary text that might avoid the charge of evading the issue of the ultimate vacuity of language and of the identities, cultural and personal, that are formed out of language and other sign-systems, is a postmodernist type of text which self-consciously builds into its own imaginative texture a view of language comparable to that formulated by poststructuralist theorists.

Once the point about the emptiness had been made it could only go on being made in relation to more literary texts and with varying degrees of sophistication and complexity. The problem was one of repetition and predictability, since it was possible to know at the outset pretty much what would be found at the end of each poststructuralist critical exercise. It is in reaction against the formalist tendency in much poststructuralist, as well as in earlier, criticism – a tendency, that is, to consider the language of texts in detachment from their social and historical contexts – that a number of critics since the early 1980s have begun to look at the discourses of literary texts in relation to the variety of discourses at play in the historical period and the culture within which the literary text was situated. There has been, in short, a new emphasis on the social and historical context of literary works. This emphasis is not simply an old-fashioned manner of looking at the historical 'background' of literary texts as if that 'background' were a stable, unchanging, objective fact. It is an emphasis which incorporates techniques learned from poststructuralism. It does not assume that texts, either literary or historical, economic or political, or whatever, transparently reflect a reality or a truth outside themselves. Instead, all texts are representations and are engaged in partly constructing the reality they are dealing with. And as such constructions both literary and other texts can be read as ideological formations which are specific to particular societies at particular phases of historical development. The ideological representations of texts – literary or otherwise – tend to serve, endorse and reproduce the power-structures, in all their complexity and internal dissensions, of any particular society at any particular time. Literature is not therefore something which can be regarded as occupying a 'trans-historical' aesthetic space, but something which must be read as subject to the discourses and ideologies of a particular time and place. The next chapter will summarize some of these historicist readings of Romantic literature in the course of pursuing the question of the relation between Enlightenment characteristics in literature on one hand, and Romantic characteristics on the other.

# 3

## ENLIGHTENMENT *AND* ROMANTIC

### POLITICS AND SPIRITUALITY

When, in his essay 'English Romanticism: The Spirit of the Age',
M.H. Abrams proposed that the Romantic poets 'were all centrally
political and social poets' (quoted p. 94), he invoked as an authority the writings of William Hazlitt. Abrams referred to the 1818
lecture 'On the Living Poets', where Hazlitt observed that 'the Lake
school of poetry . . . had its origin in the French revolution, or
rather in those . . . opinions which produced that revolution'
(quoted p. 86). As I indicated in the previous chapter, Abrams
argues that the revolutionary nature of Wordsworth's poetry is to
be understood less in directly political and more in spiritual and
aesthetic terms. In form and subject Wordsworth subverted 'a view
of poetry inherited from the Renaissance', a view which had
'assumed and incorporated a hierarchical structure of social classes'
(quoted p. 100). It was in challenging this view of poetry, in
challenging a class-based hierarchy of genres, styles and fit subjects,
that Wordsworth managed to be a political and social poet. Actual

politics were displaced into the realm of the spirit, which for Abrams remains in some sense politicized and socialized: 'Having given up the hope of revolutionizing the social and political structure, Wordsworth . . . discovered that his new calling . . . is to effect through his poetry an egalitarian revolution of the spirit' (quoted p. 100). To support this view of Wordworth's poetry Abrams quotes from Hazlitt's 1825 book *The Spirit of the Age*:

> [Wordworth's poetry] partakes of, and is carried along with, the revolutionary movement of our age: the political changes of the day were the model on which he formed and conducted his poetical experiments. His Muse . . . is a levelling one. It proceeds on a principle of equality, and strives to reduce all things to the same standard. . . .
>
> His popular, inartificial style gets rid (at a blow) of all . . . the high places of poetry. . . . We begin *de novo*, on a tabula rasa of poetry. The distinctions of rank, birth, wealth, power . . . are not to be found here. . . . The harp of Homer, the trump of Pindar and of Alcaeus, are still.
>
> (Frye 1963: 27, 61)

But Abrams does not quote those parts of the 1818 lecture 'On the Living Poets' where Hazlitt is sarcastically sceptical about the validity of seeing exact correspondences between the brute reality of the social and political world, a world where people have their heads sheared off, and the world of literary genres. Or again, he is sceptical about whether any kind of equation can be claimed between the use of capital letters in print and the real social and political powers of the aristocracy:

> Mr. Wordsworth is at the head of that which has been denominated the Lake school of poetry; a school which . . . I do not think sacred from criticism or exempt from faults. . . . Our poetical literature had, towards the close of the last century, degenerated. . . . It wanted something to stir it up, and it found

that something in the principles and events of the French revolution. . . . There was a mighty ferment in the heads of statesmen and poets, kings and people. According to the prevailing notions, all was to be natural and new. Nothing that was established was to be tolerated. All the common-place figures of poetry, tropes, allegories, personifications, with the whole heathen mythology, were instantly discarded; a classical allusion was considered as a piece of antiquated foppery; capital letters were no more allowed in print, than letters-patent of nobility were permitted in real life; kings and queens were dethroned from their rank and station in legitimate tragedy or epic poetry, as they were decapitated elsewhere; rhyme was looked upon as a relic of the feudal system, and regular meter was abolished along with regular government.

(Howe 1930–34: 161–62)

Hazlitt goes further in lampooning the social and political pretensions of the Lake Poets, when he observes how egotistical, solipsistic and, in fact, anti-communal the essential tendency of their poetry really was:

It was a time of promise, a renewal of the world and of letters; and the Deucalions, who were to perform this feat of regeneration, were the present poet-laureat [Southey] and the two authors of the Lyrical Ballads. . . . They took the same method in their new-fangled 'ballad-mongering' scheme, which Rousseau did in his prose paradoxes – of exciting attention by reversing the established standards of opinion and estimation in the world. They were for bringing poetry back to its primitive simplicity and state of nature, as he was for bringing society back to the savage state. . . . A thorough adept in this school of poetry and philanthropy is jealous of all excellence but his own. He does not even like to share his reputation with his subject; for he would have it all proceed from his own power and originality of mind. . . . He tolerates only what he himself creates; he sympathizes only with what can enter into no competition with him, with 'the bare trees and mountains bare, and grass in the green field'. He sees nothing but himself and the universe.

(Howe 1930–34: 162–63)

Hazlitt's scepticism about the correspondence between the social and political on one hand, and the poetic on the other, contrasts with Abrams' conflation of the two. Wordsworth came to discover that his 'divine "mission"' was to 'effect through his poetry an egalitarian revolution of the spirit', writes Abrams. Further,

the flash of vision [in *The Prelude*, 1805, VI. 533–36] . . . reveals that infinite longings are inherent in the human spirit. . . . The militancy of overt political action has been transformed into the paradox of spiritual quietism. . . . hope has been shifted from the history of mankind to the mind of the single individual, from militant external action to an imaginative act.

(quoted above, pp. 98–99)

But this shift of focus from society and practical politics to 'the mind of the single individual' can appear to some, as to Hazlitt, an anti-communal shift. In this concentration on the spiritual dimension, howsoever it is claimed to be a form of 'philanthropy', the poet may be understood, as Hazlitt says, to see 'nothing but himself and the universe'. The egotistical evasion of social and political matters, the essentially isolationist nature of an insistence on spiritual reality as the primary reality, was commented on a few years after Hazlitt by Karl Marx in his comments on religion. In his 1844 essay 'On the Jewish Question' Marx observed that

Man emancipates himself from religion *politically* by banishing it from the sphere of public law into that of private right. Religion is no longer the spirit of the *state* where man behaves as a species-being in community with other men. . . . It has become the spirit of *civil society*, of the sphere of egoism. . . . It is no longer the essence of *community*, but the essence of *distinction*. Religion has become what it was *originally*, an expression of the *separation* of man from his *communal* nature, from himself and from other men. It now remains only an abstract recognition of a particular oddity, of a *private whim*, of caprice.

(Kamenka 1983: 103–104)

Again in 1844, in the Introduction to his 'Contribution to the Critique of Hegel's Philosophy of Right', Marx noted that

The basis of irreligious criticism is: *man makes religion*, religion does not make man. Religion, indeed, is the self-consciousness and the self-esteem of the man who has not yet found himself or who has already lost himself. But *man* is not an abstract being crouching outside the world. Man is man's *world*, the state, society. This state and this society produce religion, which is an *inverted consciousness* of the world because state and society are an *inverted world*. Religion is the general theory of this world, its encyclopedia, its logic in popular form, its spiritualistic *point d'honneur*, its enthusiasm, its moral sanction, its solemn complement, and the general ground for the consummation and justification of this world. It is the *ghostly realization* of the human essence, ghostly because the *human essence* possesses no true reality. The struggle against religion is therefore indirectly the struggle against *that world* whose spritual aroma is religion.

Religious suffering is at once the *expression* of real suffering and the *protest* against real suffering. Religion is the sigh of the oppressed creature, the heart of a heartless world, just as it is the spirit of spiritless conditions. It is the *opium* of the people.

The overcoming of religion as the *illusory* happiness of the people is the demand for their real happiness.

(Kamenka 1983: 115)

Whatever Wordsworth's political radicalism in the early 1790s – in *A Letter to the Bishop of Llandaff*, for example – his poetry in the early nineteenth century may indeed be seen, as M.H. Abrams writes, to purvey the values of 'spritual quietism'. Quietist senti-ments underpin, for example, his 'Ode: Intimations of Immortality From Recollections of Early Childhood', which was composed from 1802 to 1804 and was published in 1807 in his *Poems, in Two Volumes*:

> The thought of our past years in me doth breed
> Perpetual benedictions: not indeed
> For that which is most worthy to be blest;
> Delight and liberty, the simple creed
> Of Childhood . . .
>     Not for these I raise
>     The song of thanks and praise;
>     But for those obstinate questionings
>     Of sense and outward things . . .
>     But for those first affections,
>     Those shadowy recollections,
>         Which, be they what they may,
> Are yet the fountain light of all our day
> Are yet a master light of all our seeing;
>     Uphold us, cherish us, and make
> Our noisy years seem moments in the being
> Of the eternal Silence: truths that wake,
>         To perish never . . .
>     Hence, in a season of calm weather,
>         Though inland far we be,
> Our Souls have sight of that immortal sea
>         Which brought us hither.

> (136–40, 142–45, 151–59, 164–67; Gill 1984: 301)

It is possible to see this kind of quietism or mysticism, seductively beautiful as it is, as an expression of what Marx called 'the *separa-tion* of man from his *communal* nature', as something which *culpably* avoids engagement with social and political reality. From the perspective of Marx's comment that religion constitutes *illusory*

happiness at the expense of real happiness, someone who main-
tains the illusion of religious or spiritual happiness conspires
actively and selfishly against the real happiness of the people. In
this sense Wordsworth remains, as Abrams would have him, a
'political and social' poet, with the difference that his implicit
political ideology is now not revolutionary but, as Marx would
have it, conservative.

The idea that an emphasis on inner, spiritual concerns at the
expense of external, social concerns is automatically a politically
conservative emphasis may be used to read a great deal of
Wordsworth's nineteenth-century productions, particularly the
*Prelude* of 1805 and *The Excursion* of 1814. One of the lines of
development traced in the autobiographical narrative of *The
Prelude* is Wordsworth's gradual shift from external to internal
modes of fulfilment. Wordsworth tells us how he had enthusiasti-
cally supported the French Revolution in its early days:

> Bliss was it in that dawn to be alive,
> But to be young was very heaven! O times . . .
> When Reason seemed the most to assert her rights.
>
> (1805, X. 692–93, 697; Wordsworth, Abrams and Gill 1979: 396)

But the terrors of 1793, when the Jacobins under Robespierre
executed not only aristocrats but also large numbers of Girondins,
the more moderate revolutionaries, had disgusted Wordsworth:

> I scarcely had one night of quiet sleep,
> Such ghastly visions had I of despair,
> And tyranny, and implements of death,
> And long orations which in dreams I pleaded
> Before unjust tribunals, with a voice
> Labouring, a brain confounded, and a sense
> Of treachery and desertion in the place
> The holiest that I knew of – my own soul.
>
> (1805, X. 373–80; Wordsworth, Abrams and Gill 1979: 378)

From such confusion of soul at the souring of the political and social revolution Wordsworth turned for consolation to nature and to contemplation of the depths of his own mind. In the thirteenth book of *The Prelude* we find him asking and asserting:

> Oh, who is he that hath his whole life long
> Preserved, enlarged, this freedom in himself? –
> For this alone is genuine liberty.
>
> (1805, XIII. 120–22; Wordsworth, Abrams and Gill 1979: 464)

But what really *is* this inner freedom? The term freedom begins to lose the socio-political meaning of equality, liberty and fraternity when we discover that it is really the 'invisible' world, the realm of God, that is meant, and not the world of actual phenomena, people and events. The 'freedom' Wordsworth is eulogizing here is the freedom of what a few lines earlier he has called 'higher minds' (1805, XIII. 90; Wordsworth, Abrams and Gill 1979: 462) to interact imaginatively with the external world, above all with nature. And the point about this interaction is that it is free of social constraint and is leading all the time beyond the phenomenal world. Wordsworth observes how 'higher minds' are not slaves to the sensory world but are stimulated by that world to see beyond it:

> in a world of life they live,
> By sensible impressions not enthralled,
> But quickened, rouzed, and made thereby more fit
> To hold communion with the invisible world.
> Such minds are truly from the Deity,
> For they are powers; and hence the highest bliss
> That can be known is theirs.
>
> (1805, XIII. 102–108; Wordsworth, Abrams and Gill 1979: 464)

At the end of the 1805 *Prelude* Wordsworth claims he is able to instruct others in truth about 'the mind of man' (1805, XIII. 446; Wordsworth, Abrams and Gill 1979: 482). But the claim to be able to generalize about an universal 'mind of man' is vitiated by the fact

that at points in *The Prelude* he has not been purveying an egalitarian notion of a mind common to all human beings but rather
has been celebrating what he thinks of as 'higher minds'. More
important, it is apparent that what is distinctive about these higher
minds is that, according to a certain way of looking at the matter,
they are not really human at all. What is significant is the extent to
which they can be shown to be grounded in and are capable of
apprehending an unearthly reality: 'Such minds are truly from the
Deity'. Are other minds, then, not from the Deity? In thus celebrating a specialized humanity it could be said that Wordsworth is
paradoxically celebrating the inhuman. The focus on the high
value of communing with the non-visible world stands in sharp
contrast with Wordsworth's recollection, in the tenth book of the
1805 *Prelude*, that those who supported the French Revolution at
its outset were not utopian idealists but people who knew

> the very world which is the world
> Of all of us, the place in which, in the end,
> We find our happiness, or not at all.
>
> (1805, X. 725–27; Wordsworth, Abrams and Gill 1979: 398)

Wordsworth's shift to identifying happiness with the individual's
apprehension of the invisible world stands liable to the Marxist
charge that this is simply an '*illusory* happiness' which bears
conservative, even reactionary political implications.

Wordsworth's redefinition and interiorization of the term
'freedom', so that it no longer defines anything in the social and
political arena but is to be associated with the 'genuine liberty'
of the inner self, corresponds suggestively with the increasingly
reactionary nature of the governing powers in Britain from the
mid-1790s onwards. In May 1792 a Royal Proclamation against
Seditious Writings was issued and in December Thomas Paine
(who had already escaped to France) was outlawed, and *Rights of
Man* censored as seditious libel. From 1793 Britain was at war
with Revolutionary France and in 1794 William Pitt's government

suspended the Habeas Corpus Act and began proceedings against radical societies such as the London Corresponding Society and the London Society for Constitutional Information. Luminaries of these societies, Thomas Hardy, John Thelwall and John Horne Tooke, were arrested and accused of high treason. Anti-Jacobin newspapers were published which pilloried radical sentiment and government spies harassed individuals thought to hold radical sympathies. In 1797, when Wordsworth and Coleridge were living in Somerset and when fears of a West Country invasion by the French were intense, a government agent was despatched to monitor the two poets who were suspected for a while of being spies for the enemy. In the 1805 *Prelude* Wordsworth disdainfully remembers the repression of Pitt's government:

> As vermin working out of reach, they leagued
> Their strength perfidiously to undermine
> Justice, and make an end of liberty.
>
> (1805, X. 654–56; Wordsworth, Abrams and Gill 1979: 394)

Nevertheless, the spiritual liberty that *The Prelude* as a whole endorses can read as a conservative evasion of social and political libertarian demands. Political conservatism becomes more explicit in Wordsworth's later poem *The Excursion*.

*The Excursion* was first published in 1814, the year before the British finally defeated the French, now led by Napoleon, at the Battle of Waterloo. *The Excursion*, in nine books, is the second part of the grand three-part poem entitled *The Recluse* which Wordsworth planned but never completed (*The Prelude* was initially thought of as an appendage to *The Recluse*). *The Excursion* has a dramatic structure with four main characters: the poet, the Wanderer, the Solitary and the Pastor. The last three hold long discourses – to use the words of the Preface to the poem – 'On Man, on Nature, and on Human Life' (1; de Selincourt and Darbishire 1972: 3). The Solitary is a man who had held out great hopes for the renovation of human kind during the early years of the French Revolution but who has sunk into a kind of despair at the failure of revolutionary hopes. The Wanderer seeks to save him from his despair. He too had shared feelings of revolutionary optimism but he now sees that plans to transform society are false dreams. Instead, he characterizes those dreams almost as sins of pride, indulged in by men who thought they knew more than all preceding generations of human kind:

> So doth he advise
> Who shared at first the illusion; but was soon
> Cast from the pedestal of pride by shocks
> Which Nature gently gave, in woods and fields;
> Nor unreproved by Providence, thus speaking
> To the inattentive children of the world:
> 'Vain-glorious Generation! what new powers
> On you have been conferred? what gifts, withheld
> From your progenitors, have ye received,
> Fit recompense of new desert?'
>
> (IV. 272–81; de Selincourt and Darbishire 1972: 117)

Against hopes for 'social man' (IV. 261; de Selincourt and Darbishire 1972: 117) the Wanderer asserts that true fulfilment is to be found in retreating from society into solitary contemplation amidst natural scenes and in holding 'Faith absolute in God' (IV. 22; de Selincourt and Darbishire 1972: 110). His religious prescription is slightly reminiscent of *The Prelude* but the politically conservative implications of that prescription are spelled out in *The Excursion*. In Book IX the Wanderer, having discoursed about the highest principle he can think of, 'the Soul of all the worlds' (IX. 15; de Selincourt and Darbishire 1972: 287), goes on to bewail the disintegration of old social orders in Europe as a whole:

> from Calpe's sunburnt cliffs
> To the flat margin of the Baltic sea,
> Long-reverenced titles cast away as weeds;

Laws overturned; and territory split,
Like fields of ice rent by the polar wind.

(IX. 336–40; de Selincourt and Darbishire 1972: 297)

The Wanderer has the seal of authorial approval in *The Excursion* and his Burkean complaint at the overturning of old titles and laws contrasts vividly with the revolutionary sentiment of Wordsworth's 1793 *Letter to the Bishop of Llandaff.* By 1814 Wordsworth is no longer the radical. He is now preaching, through the lips of the Wanderer, the need for people to return to their hearth-fires and to live ordered lives, submitting to traditional notions of virtue, prudence and piety:

the more do we require
The discipline of virtue; order else
Cannot subsist, nor confidence, nor peace.
Thus, duties rising out of good possest
And prudent caution needful to avert
Impending evil, equally require
That the whole people should be taught and trained.
So shall licentiousness and black resolve
Be rooted out, and virtuous habits take
Their place; and genuine piety descend,
Like an inheritance, from age to age.

(IX. 352–62; de Selincourt and Darbishire 1972: 297–98)

In contrast with the more mystical religious tendencies of, say, 'Tintern Abbey' or the 1805 *Prelude*, Wordsworth advances in *The Excursion* a much more orthodox Christian faith. He compounds this with a eulogy – couched in an imperialist rhetoric – of the existing British state. The world will look to Britain for leadership and Britain must look, the Wanderer declares, to its glorious future:

O for the coming of that glorious time
When, prizing knowledge as her noblest wealth
And best protection, this imperial Realm,

> While she exacts allegiance, shall admit
> An obligation, on her part, to *teach*
> Them who are born to serve her and obey . . .
> – Vast the circumference of hope – and ye
> Are at its centre, British lawgivers . . .
>                     Your Country must complete
> Her glorious destiny.

> (IX. 293–98, 398–99, 407–408; de Selincourt and
> Darbishire 1972: 295, 299)

On the connection between Romanticism and imperialism Marlon B. Ross has written, in an article entitled 'Romantic Quest and Conquest', that:

> In a very real sense the Romantics . . . help prepare England for its imperial destiny. They help teach the English to universalize the experience of 'I', a self-conscious task for Wordsworth, whose massive philosophical poem *The Recluse* sets out to organize the universe by celebrating the universal validity of parochial English values.

> (Mellor 1988: 31)

Not surprisingly, when Percy Bysshe and Mary Shelley read *The Excursion* in September 1814, Mary wrote in her journal: 'Shelley . . . brings home Wordworth's "Excursion", of which we read a part, much disappointed. He is a slave' (Jones 1947: 15). Wordsworth's slavishness had already been publicly apparent in a little poem which he wrote in 1802 and published in 1807. The drift of thought in 'London, 1802' again contrasts with the republican anger of the 1793 *Letter to the Bishop of Llandaff*, where 'little is thought of snatching the bread' from the mouths of the poor in order 'to eke out the "*necessary* splendor" of nobility' (quoted above, p. 34). In 'London, 1802' the homely hearthside virtues of a feudal order of society are eulogized and equated with a condition of inner, private fulfilment:

Milton! thou should'st be living at this hour:
England hath need of thee: she is a fen
Of stagnant waters: altar, sword and pen,
Fireside, the heroic wealth of hall and bower,
Have forfeited their ancient English dower
Of inward happiness.

(1–6; Gill 1984: 286)

## CONSERVATIVE NOVELISTS

The 'ancient' and 'heroic wealth of hall' is the theme of a novelist who is not often spoken of in the same breath as Wordsworth. But Jane Austen was writing and publishing at roughly the same time as the poet. While she made a study of sensibility in *Sense and Sensibility* (1811), Austen is not identified with celebrations of the imagination in the Romantic sense. The political import of her novels has long been recognized as conservative. And in that respect her novels have something in common with the increasing conservatism evident in Wordworth's early nineteenth-century poetry. The heroine of Austen's *Mansfield Park*, which was published in the same year as *The Excursion*, is Fanny Price, whose mother made a 'bad' marriage and, accordingly, lives a decidedly lower middle-class life in Portsmouth. Because of her parents' poverty Fanny is brought up by her aunt who has made a 'good' marriage to Sir Thomas Bertram of Mansfield Park. Sir Thomas is presented as a trustworthy and fair man who at a certain point in the story of the inhabitants of Mansfield Park leaves the great house on business (while the business is in Antigua, when wealth would have been built on the appalling slave-economy of the Caribbean, no detailed study is made of the *nature* of his affairs). During Sir Thomas' absence there comes into the world of Mansfield Park a glittering couple from London: Henry Crawford and his sister Mary. These two, along with Sir Thomas' eldest son Tom, his two sisters and certain others, undertake to stage a disharmonious play, a curious amalgam of the tragic and the comic, in the billiard room of the great house, using Sir Thomas' own private room as a green room. The point is parodic. The staging of the play and particularly the use of Sir Thomas' room mocks the dignity and authority of the old aristocrat. Order is restored only when Sir Thomas returns unexpectedly early just as the play is being acted. Austen's message is that the ancient authorities and virtues of England are in danger of being forfeited, of being turned into a farce. The shallowness of the Crawfords and their association with London identify the capital with new money, with moral licence and superficial fashionableness, with social forces that were putting the old order of England at risk. The order of Mansfield Park is also contrasted favourably with the disorder apparent in Fanny's parents' household in Portsmouth. The point here seems frankly a matter of class snobbery. Fanny finds her real parents' home:

> in almost every respect, the very reverse of what she could have wished. It was the abode of noise, disorder, and impropriety. Nobody was in their right place, nothing was done as it ought to be.

> (Austen 1980: 381)

In *Mansfield Park* Austen is endorsing the idea of social order and degree, a civil state where everyone knows their place and everything is done in accordance with that knowledge. Such a traditional society is also a patriarchal system and Austen shows Fanny throughout as self-effacing, passive and submissive. In the end these supposedly feminine virtues are shown as paying off since Edmund, the younger clergyman son of Sir Thomas, falls in love with Fanny and the two marry, bringing Fanny fully into the orbit of Mansfield Park which she has come to regard as her true home. The conclusion to the novel is a celebration of rural Tory values which steadfastly refuses to pay detailed attention to contemporary phenomena such as the war with France or the fact that Britain stood on the disorientating threshold of mass industrialization and urbanization.

The novels of Walter Scott also purvey a branch of conservative thought in that they endorse the established British state of the early nineteenth century. In *Waverley*, another work first published in the same year as *The Excursion*, Scott takes as his subject the Jacobite rebellion of 1745 against the Hanoverian rulers of England and Scotland. Scott's hero, Edward Waverley, is a young man who goes into Scotland with the Hanoverian army. While in the Highlands he falls in love with a Jacobite sympathizer, Flora Mac-Ivor, and he switches his allegiance from the Hanoverian to the Jacobite cause. At the Battle of Prestonpans, now fighting on the side of the Jacobites, he saves the life of Colonel Talbot, an English officer, who secures Edward's pardon once the Jacobites are finally defeated at the Battle of Culloden. Throughout the novel the Jacobites represent the old feudal order of Scotland. They are presented as attractive in their fierce clan loyalties but at the same time their society is viewed as primitive and obsolescent. Edward's attachment to their cause is seen as a symptom of his youth and immaturity. The Hanoverian world of the novel is presented as the new order of Britain. It represents the future with which Britons at the time *Waverley* was published were living. In its most positive aspect it is presented as reasonable and accommodating and the novel recommends it as the world of maturity and realism. It is the world which Edward rejoins after he has put away childish things and passed beyond his Jacobite sympathies. Towards the end of the novel we find Edward, hiding in Cumberland as the Jacobite rebellion is reduced to tatters, beginning to come to terms with his own and the state's maturity:

> Most devoutly did he hope . . . that it might never again be his lot to draw his sword in civil conflict. . . . he felt himself entitled to say firmly, though perhaps with a sigh, that the romance of his life was ended, and that its real history had now commenced.
>
> (Scott 1986: 283)

## HISTORICISM AND ROMANTICISM

Wordsworth's place amongst writers in the early nineteenth century who, in their different ways, supported the conservative British order has led some commentators since the beginning of the 1980s to build on the work of earlier historically minded critics such as Carl Woodring and David Erdman (see, for example, Woodring 1970 and Erdman 1954) and to re-read Wordworth's poetry for its sometimes hidden political connotations. I have space to note only a couple of examples of this historicist criticism and I shall begin with observations on the poem 'Alice Fell', which Wordsworth first published in 1807.

The story of 'Alice Fell', which is based on a true report by Wordsworth's acquaintance Robert Graham, is simple enough: the first person speaker of the poem tells of his meeting with a young girl who is extremely distressed because her cloak has caught and torn in the wheel of the coach in which they are both travelling. The girl is an orphaned waif who travels on the outside at the back of the coach:

> suddenly I seemed to hear
> A moan, a lamentable sound . . .
>
> Said I, alighting on the ground,
> 'What can it be, this piteous moan?'
> And there a little Girl I found,
> Sitting behind the Chaise, alone.
>
> 'My Cloak!' the word was last and first,
> And loud and bitterly she wept . . .
>
> 'What ails you, Child?' She sobbed, 'Look here!'
> I saw it in the wheel entangled,
> A weather beaten Rag as e'er
> From any garden scare-crow dangled.

> (3–4, 17–22, 25–28; Gill 1984: 241)

The speaker takes the girl inside the coach and attempts to comfort her, but her grief at the loss of her tattered cloak seems inconsolable. In the end, when they have reached their destination, the speaker gives a local innkeeper money to buy Alice Fell a new cloak:

> 'And let it be a duffil grey,
> As warm a cloak as man can sell!'
> Proud Creature was she the next day,
> The little Orphan, Alice Fell!
>
> (57–60; Gill 1984: 242)

Commenting on the poem in his 1964 book on Wordsworth, *Wordsworth's Poetry 1787–1814*, Geoffrey Hartman saw it only in interior, spiritual terms, as a study of the way in which obsessive grief may be a form of self-protection against an even greater sense of alienation or despair:

> The poems that caused Wordsworth's notoriety, and which are not, of course, restricted to *Lyrical Ballads* (consider 'Alice Fell' . . . ), are basically similar in showing us people cleaving to one thing or idea with a tenaciousness both pathetic and frightening. This physical or imaginative cleaving, which is the central passion, results from a separation, if we use the word in its strongest sense, as when the mystics speak of a separation from God. . . . Wordsworth's sufferers. . . . cleave to one thing or idea in order to be saved from a still deeper sense of separation. It does not matter whether a child is deprived of its tattered cloak or a woman of child and lover – the wound that opens is always the same, and even when the loss is ordinary, the passion is extraordinary, and points to so deep and personal a sorrow that we call it natural only to dignify human nature.
>
> (Hartman 1977: 143)

Subtle as Hartman's reading is, it misses a point highlighted by David Simpson in his 1987 book *Wordsworth's Historical*

*Imagination*, which is that it is possible to detect in the interaction between speaker and child a historically specific vocabulary that touches the contemporary late eighteenth and early nineteenth-century debate 'about the rights and wrongs of charity as against a systematic public policy for the relief of the vagrant poor' (Simpson 1987: 178). Simpson refers to the tenth stanza of 'Alice Fell', when the child has been taken into the coach by the speaker:

> She sate like one past all relief;
> Sob after sob she forth did send
> In wretchedness, as if her grief
> Could never, never, have an end.

> (37–40; Gill 1984: 242)

Simpson says of this stanza that:

> She seems to be beyond 'relief' – a very important word, for in contemporary discourse it was the one always used to describe the general, public enterprise of assisting the poor. (*The Oxford English Dictionary* records it as applying specifically to the Poor Laws and the parish doles, but only up to 1865). The reader of 1807 would have 'perceived' the charge that this word carries.

> (Simpson 1987: 179)

The contemporary 'charge' of this word, lost to readers in the late twentieth century, leads Simpson to argue that in the tenth stanza, as well as recording his inability to assuage her grief, the speaker is suggesting that Alice – and perhaps through her, emblematically, 'the vagrant poor in general' (Simpson 1987: 179) – lie beyond the scope of systematized public aid. Instead, the poem seems to approve of the individual act of charity as something that restores not merely material well-being, the new, protective cloak, but also a sense of pride to Alice Fell. Simpson proposes that in Wordsworth's apparent endorsement of the speaker's act of charity it is possible to trace 'a Burkean approval of the practice of private charity over the case for public relief' (Simpson 1987: 180). Simpson's mention of Edmund Burke leads him into a further point about the iconography of 'Alice Fell'. The poem turns on the matter of Alice Fell's protective garment, her cloak. Simpson observes that the matter of clothing was itself at the time fraught with political resonances:

> the debate or choice between nakedness and clothing was a feature of the 'political' rhetoric of the times. . . . Rousseau . . . identified civic virtue with nakedness. . . . Burke, on the contrary, suggests that clothing is what makes us most creatively human, redeeming us as far as anything can from the indignity of our fallen state. . . . Clothing turns necessity to virtue. . . . Against the republican image of naked or minimally clothed virtue, apparent in the literature, art and fashion of the revolutionary period, Burke offers a recourse to the necessity of robes and furred gowns. In Wordsworth's poem, Alice has a brief experience of naked and shivering nature, and is restored to a dignity in her own estimation.
>
> (Simpson 1987: 181)

Reading the poem within the discourses of the time it is possible to read 'Alice Fell' not in the manner of Geoffrey Hartman, as dealing with some historically transcendent state of the human soul, but, as Simpson says, as a conservative political allegory:

> a Burkean allegory telling of the reclaiming of one potentially fierce and wild (*fell*) and fallen (as a human being) into the society of property, possession and self-esteem. . . . the conversion of a potentially exiled and accusatory figure, and thus a prototypic revolutionary, into a solid Burkean citizen.
>
> (Simpson 1987: 181)

Wordsworth's unstated conservatism is the subject of another new historicist study by Marjorie Levinson, who goes back as far as 1798 and to 'Tintern Abbey' to make her case (*Wordsworth's Great*

*Period Poems. Four Essays*, 1986). In the course of an elaborately detailed argument about the poem Levinson picks up on a point that has frequently been made by Wordsworth's commentators, which is that there is in 'Tintern Abbey' no description of the abbey at all. The full title of the work would perhaps not encourage us to expect such a description: 'Lines written a few miles above Tintern Abbey, on revisiting the banks of the Wye during a tour, July 13, 1798'. Wordsworth certainly did visit the abbey itself during his walking tour with his sister Dorothy along the Wye valley from the 10th to the 13th July 1798 (Moorman 1968: 401–407). But the title of the poem could be taken quite literally: this was a poem written on the River Wye in the vicinity of but not actually at Tintern Abbey. Even allowing this, however, the mention of the abbey in the title does raise questions. Levinson asks: 'Why would a writer call attention to a famous ruin and then studiously ignore it, as it were repudiating its material and historical facticity? Why not situate his utterance in the bower or dell and avoid the cynosure altogether?' (Levinson 1986: 15). The answer Levinson offers is that Tintern Abbey signified two different and mutually contradictory things for Wordsworth in 1798. On the one hand, the abbey, which was once an institutionally religious place, is now, in its picturesquely ruined state, still potentially a space to be associated with retreat and meditation, a 'sacred spot' offering the individual an 'escape from the social body and the historical moment' (Levinson 1986: 33). This is certainly how contemporary writers – often influenced by notions of the sublime as something associated with religious awe – viewed Tintern Abbey. Levinson quotes from a 1799 diary published in 1810: 'the village and abbey of Tintern: a delicious retreat, most felicitously chosen ... for the purposes of religious meditation and retirement. ... the Abbey-Church ... magical and sublime effect' (Levinson 1986: 31). For Wordsworth, Levinson suggests, the ruined abbey would have carried just such a spiritual connotation. The problem was that in 1798 Tintern Abbey was also associated with something very different. The town of Tintern, some half a mile from the abbey, had become a centre for iron working, the River Wye was infested with commercial traffic, and the abbey itself was host to a substantial population of vagrants, a population of the unemployed and dispossessed. The scene is described in William Gilpin's guidebook, *Observations on the River Wye* (1792), with which Wordsworth was apparently familiar (Moorman 1968: 402):

> Among other things in this scene of desolation, the poverty and wretchedness of the inhabitants are remarkable. They occupy little huts, raised among the ruins of the monastery and seem to have no employment, but begging.
>
> The country around Tintern Abbey hath been described as a solitary, tranquil scene: but its immediate environs only are meant. Within half a mile of it are carried on great iron-works; which introduce noise and bustle. . . . Hitherto the river had been clear, and splendid. . . . But its water now became ouzy and discoloured.
>
> (Levinson 1986: 31)

Wordworth's problem, according to Levinson, was that while the abbey might be taken to signify spiritual retreat, it had come simultaneously to signify a deeply problematical social reality, which Wordsworth did not want to acknowledge, and so the abbey is advertized in the poem's title but avoided in the poem itself:

> Rather than invest Tintern Abbey with . . . charm or gleam, Wordsworth consecrates a nearby stretch of farm and woodland, ascribing to this landscape the power to prompt a devotion finer – more abstract – than even 'la sentiment des ruines'. He does this for two associated reasons. First, the actual impression made by Tintern, town and Abbey, defeats even Wordsworth's genius for imaginative alchemy. Tintern Abbey is not just another religious house wasted by time. . . . Tintern's

> devaluation is the effect of irresistible socioeconomic forces allegorically and *immediately* inscribed in the town, along the river banks, and within the ruin itself. . . .
>
> in 1798, in *England* – felt at that time to be economically and militarily endangered – the spectacle of a national monument overrun with what looked to be a morally and materially unfixed class could not be taken lightly, especially by a man not entirely easy with his egalitarianism, a man already homesick for the memorialized landscapes of his childhood.
>
> (Levinson 1986: 35)

And Wordsworth is primarily concerned to effect in 'Tintern Abbey' an erasure of anything to do with socio-economic forces: 'the primary poetic action is the suppression of the social. . . . The success or failure of the visionary poem turns on its ability to hide its omission of the historical' (Levinson 1986: 37, 39).

The landscape that *is* described in the poem is a curiously generalized one which admits of no direct engagement with the local topography of Tintern – a topography brutally marked by particular social and historical phenomena. One point at which Wordsworth does seem to register the dispossessed population of the Tintern area is when, at the end of the opening landscape description, he notes:

> these pastoral farms
> Green to the very door; and wreathes of smoke
> Sent up, in silence, from among the trees,
> With some uncertain notice, as might seem,
> Of vagrant dwellers in the houseless woods,
> Or of some hermit's cave, where by his fire
> The hermit sits alone.
>
> (17–23; Brett and Jones 1976: 113–14)

The problem is that even this notice of 'vagrant dwellers' is seeking to hide the harsh facts of beggary and vagrancy. Referring to the expression 'as might seem,/Of vagrant dwellers in the houseless woods', Levinson observes:

> The curiosity of the phrase is, of course, its gratuitous allusion to the vagrants. The strictly notional being of these figures ('as might seem . . . ') marks an attempt to elide the confessed factual intelligence. Or, while the passage explicitly associates the smoke with the cosy pastoral farms, and situates the image as an instance of natural supernaturalism, the 'surmise' identifies the smoke as the effects of charcoal burning. More to the point, it identifies those idealized vagrants – a sort of metonymic slide toward the hermit/poet – as the actual charcoal burners who migrated according to the wood supply and the market. Or, more simply, Wordsworth reverses objective and subjective knowledges: he presents the real vagrants as hypostatized (archetypal) figures, and positions the scene all gratulant – an idea *tout court* – as unmediated sensory impression. Moreover, we observe that by equating the wanderers with the hermit – one who possesses even less than they but one whose spirit is inversely enriched and exalted – Wordsworth further discredits the factual knowledge hiding in his representation. Following the text, we forget that hermits choose their poverty; vagrants suffer it.
>
> (Levinson 1986: 43)

What is happening in 'Tintern Abbey', Levinson argues, is a symptom of a shift in Wordsworth's thought, a shift away from the radical political position of the earlier 1790s. 'Tintern Abbey' as a whole, with its idealization of the self and of nature, and its refusal to countenance the evidence of industrial despoliation and of social underprivilege

> marks a swerve from an Enlightenment humanitarianism (an engaged, ambitious, practically objectified orientation) and a turn toward a more theoretical, disinterested, and spiritually

focused philanthropic mode (roughly, Romantic sympathy).
Wordsworth's 'transposition' of enthusiasm seems also to
indicate a degree of uneasiness with the aggressively political
persona he had established in the early verse.

(Levinson 1986: 19–20)

What 'Tintern Abbey' dramatizes, according to this kind of
reading, is a contrast between radical political attitudes belonging
to the Enlightenment and the more inwardly focused, socially
evasive and conservative thought of Romanticism proper. I
shall return at the end of this chapter to the use of the terms
Enlightenment and Romantic. For the moment I want to proceed
by commenting briefly on the way in which other writers, whom
I mentioned in the first chapter as having had radical bearings in
their youth, turned to politically more conservative positions
in the early nineteenth century.

Coleridge moved towards an attitude that may be described as
reactionary. One of the reasons for this shift was that as the 1790s
developed, the radical movement, which originally had deep roots
in the dissenting religious community, tended to become identified with the secularism and atheism of the French rationalists.
One of the most influential of French rationalist works on the
British radical movement was Constantin Volney's (1757–1820)
*Les Ruines* (1791), a book which saw religion as superstition and
superstition as a form of tyranny which reason would necessarily
overthrow in its attempt to establish freedom, equality and justice.
This kind of rationalist scepticism about religion appeared in the
work of British writers, such as William Godwin's *Political Justice*
of 1793 or Paine's *The Age of Reason* (1794–95). The increasing
association of the British radical movement with rational scepticism presented a problem for Coleridge, since he was a Christian.
Coleridge's unbroken religious faith was one of the things that
pushed him away from the radical interest and towards the conservative camp that maintained belief in the importance of social

hierarchy and of religion and the church. As Paul Hamilton has acutely observed, the later Coleridge 'supports theological and political systems in a way which helps explain the increasing coincidence in European Romanticism of orthodoxy in religion and conservatism in politics' (Hamilton 1983: 186). By 1817, in his second *Lay Sermon,* Coleridge was associating the idea of liberty not with the principle of revolution but with feudalism and the church: 'To the Feudal system we owe the *forms,* to the Church the *substance* of our liberty' (White 1972: 215). Coleridge's prose works of the early nineteenth century such as the *Lay Sermons* argued for a religious revival to be led by the upper classes.

This argument was in part conditioned by Coleridge's absorption in German ideas. Coleridge had visited Germany with Wordsworth in 1798–99 and in the course of his *Biographia Literaria* of 1817 he acknowledged his indebtedness to the thought of Immanuel Kant (1724–1804) and associated German idealist philosophers. As I noted earlier, his 1812–13 lectures on literature had displayed his indebtedness – for the distinction between classical and Romantic – to A.W. Schlegel. A.W. Schlegel and his brother Friedrich (1772–1829), who together produced the periodical *Das Athenäum* (1798–1800) which in 1798 contained, in Fragment 116, a famous definition of Romantic poetry by Friedrich, were prime movers in the definition of Romanticism in Germany. But it is difficult to describe German Romanticism as having been politically radical. It is better characterized as having been, broadly speaking, a counter-revolutionary phenomenon which reacted against the rationalist and materialist tendencies of Enlightenment and Revolutionary France. It stressed the need for a revival of religion and made a cult of introversion. In its opposition to the classical taste of Republican France it made an ideal of mediaeval sensibility and aesthetic form. German Romanticism has been characterized by Logan Pearsall Smith as 'a school of wild poets and Catholic reactionaries' (Smith 1925: 85).

The reactionariness of Coleridge manifests itself in the hostility he shows in chapter 22 of the *Biographia Literaria* towards Wordsworth's contributions to the *Lyrical Ballads*. Coleridge objects to Wordworth's dealing – 'in an elevated poem' (Shawcross 1907: II. 104) – with common objects and the lower ranks of society. In the *Biographia* Coleridge has travelled quite some way from the sympathies he had expressed in one of his own contributions to *Lyrical Ballads*, 'The Dungeon' (see p. 10). His objection to the subversion of distinctions between the social ranks in Wordsworth's contributions to *Lyrical Ballads* surfaces again when he comments negatively on a comparable subversion in certain late eighteenth-century drama:

> the whole secret of the modern Jacobinical drama . . . and of all its popularity, consists in the confusion and subversion of the natural order of things in their causes and effects: namely, in the excitement of surprise by representing the qualities of liberality, refined feeling, and a nice sense of honor . . . in persons and in classes where experience teaches us least to expect them.
>
> (Shawcross 1907: II. 192–93)

Coleridge's later *Aids to Reflection* (1825) and *On the Constitution of the Church and State* (1830) continued to advance a vision of British society as ideally aristocratic and theocratic. Indeed, so far to the right did Coleridge swing that John Barrell has spoken of *On the Constitution of the Church and State* as being, 'with Burke's *Reflections on the Revolution in France*':

> one of the few classic works of conservative thought in English, and one which unites two remarkable traditions of political theory: that of Hooker and such early seventeenth century eulogists of English Common Law as Sir Edward Coke and Sir John Davies, and that of the Romantic conservatism of Herder and his followers in Germany. . . . *On the Constitution of the Church and State* is a work of that tradition of Romantic conservatism which emerged as a reaction to the ideals of the Enlightenment.
>
> (Barrell 1972: viii–ix)

In his prose works Coleridge was to have a considerable influence on essentially conservative Victorian intellectual societies such as the Cambridge Apostles and on conservative religious tendencies such as the powerful Oxford Movement; as well as on individual Victorian sages such as Matthew Arnold and John Henry Newman. Coleridge's prose writings played, in other words, an important part in the constitution of the Victorian establishment that regarded the idea of revolution with dread: 'The red fool-fury of the Seine', as the fundamentally conservative Tennyson put it in 1850 in *In Memoriam* (CXXVII. 7; Day 1991: 217).

William Blake never had Coleridge's influence over the succeeding Victorian generation of thinkers, artists and statesmen, but from the later 1790s his work – from *Vala, or the Four Zoas* (1797) to *Jerusalem* (1804–20) – shows a retreat from direct socio-political engagement. As Marilyn Butler has observed, Blake:

> turned his attention, with *Vala, or the Four Zoas* (begun 1797), to the development of an increasingly private mythology, which is less topical than the earlier work and indeed begins to seem effectively depoliticized. ... True to the reticence of the counter-revolutionary period, Blake began to value the mystery and secrecy which in his revolutionary period he denounced as the characteristic of priestcraft.

> (Butler 1981: 51)

The movement away from society and the material world in Blake's later poems parallels the increasing emphasis on interior, spiritual reality in Wordsworth's poetry of the same period.

Another writer of erstwhile radical sympathy who turned explicitly conservative in his work was Robert Southey. Southey accepted the poet-laureateship in 1813, much to the scorn of his opponents who denounced him for apostasy, as one who had relinquished his earlier radicalism in order to gain social and financial favour. Southey's first laureate verse, the 'Carmen Triumphale for the

Commencement of the Year 1814', was a celebration of British victories against Napoleon the previous year. Like Wordsworth's *Excursion*, with its vision of Britain's 'glorious destiny' (quoted p. 138), Southey's poem eulogizes the British state, seeing it as the saviour of the world against Napoleon: 'Britain stood firm and braved his power;/Alone she fought the battles of mankind' (31–32; Fitzgerald 1909: 447). Napoleon was a tyrant who did need to be defeated, but pleasure in his defeat seems to have been associated for the likes of Southey or Wordsworth with an entire capitulation to the ways of the British state. British victory seems in their cases to be associated with a blindness to the wrongs endemic in British society; wrongs which, in their earlier days, they might have pointed out with an enthusiasm equal to that with which they now avoided the issue. As an anonymous reviewer of Southey's poem observed in the *Scourge* for February 1814:

> At the commencenment of his poetical career, Mr Southey was one of the most enthusiastic advocates for reform; a zealot in the cause of universal freedom; the determined enemy to princes and 'courts tyrannic'. . . . His early productions breathe the most pure and manly sentiments of liberty. . . . Within the last few years his tone and sentiments have undergone an extra-ordinary revolution. He is now the champion of social order, the eulogist of kings, the servant of the Prince Regent, a decided opponent of the most popular advocates of independence, and the eulogist of war!
>
> (Madden 1972: 196)

## NEW RADICALISM

Frustration at the abandonment of radicalism by writers such as Southey, Coleridge and Wordworth emerges in the writings of Thomas Love Peacock (1785–1866). Peacock was a friend of Percy Shelley. Shelley, Keats and Byron are conventionally thought of as the second generation English Romantics. In the spring and summer of 1817 Peacock was living near Shelley and his second wife Mary in Marlow, Buckinghamshire. Between April and July, Leigh Hunt (1784–1854), editor of *The Examiner*, stayed with the Shelleys, who were visited also by Mary's father William Godwin, the author of *Political Justice*. Life at the Shelleys' home, Albion House, during this period partly informs Peacock's representation of the household in his 1818 satirical novel *Nightmare Abbey*. Peacock's previous novel of 1817, *Melincourt*, had included, in the character of Mr Feathernest, a satirical portrait of Robert Southey as one who had abandoned youthful radical idealism in favour of social position and money. In *Nightmare Abbey* Peacock turned his guns on Coleridge. The target in the novel is Mr Flosky, who is characterized as one who has retreated from political radicalism into almost its exact opposite: a celebration of spiritual intro-version, obscure German metaphysics and feudal politics. Peacock's controlling metaphor of darkness and light in the following passage is a symptom of his own commitment to the Enlightenment principles he is, in effect, claiming Coleridge has foregone:

> Mystery was his mental element. He lived in the midst of that visionary world in which nothing is but what is not. . . . He had been in his youth an enthusiast for liberty, and had hailed the dawn of the French Revolution as the promise of a day that was to banish war and slavery, and every form of vice and misery, from the face of the earth. Because all this was not done, he deduced that nothing was done; and from this deduction . . . he drew a conclusion that worse than nothing was done; that the overthrow of the feudal fortresses of tyranny and superstition was the greatest calamity that had ever befallen mankind; and that their only hope now was to rake the rubbish together, and rebuild it without any of those loopholes by which the light had originally crept in. To qualify himself . . . in this laudable task, he plunged into the central opacity of Kantian metaphysics, and lay *perdu* several years in transcendental darkness, till the common daylight of common sense became intolerable to his eyes.
>
> (Garnett 1948: 360)

But it was not only the older generation of apostates that Peacock chose to satirize, for there are in *Nightmare Abbey* critical portraits, admittedly less severe than that of Coleridge, of Byron and Shelley. Peacock disliked what he saw as the current, German-influenced fashion of spiritual introversion and of melancholy alienation, all of which bore implications of political reaction. He found a German darkness and despondency infecting the earlier work of both Byron and Shelley. One particular object of attack in *Nightmare Abbey* is Byron's *Childe Harold's Pilgrimage* (1812–18), where we hear the speaker in Canto IV declaring: 'my soul wanders; I demand it back/To meditate amongst decay, and stand/A ruin amidst ruins' (IV. xxv. 1–3; Page 1970: 230). In May 1818 Peacock wrote to Shelley:

> I have almost finished *Nightmare Abbey*. I think it necessary to 'make a stand' against the 'encroachments' of black bile. The fourth canto of *Childe Harold* is really too bad. I cannot consent to be *auditor tantum* of this systematical 'poisoning' of the 'mind' of the 'reading public'.
>
> (Brett-Smith and Jones 1924–34: VIII. 193)

An aspect of Byron is portrayed in *Nightmare Abbey* in the character of the poet Mr Cypress, while an element of Shelley appears in the character of Scythrop Glowry, heir to the family seat of Nightmare Abbey. The problem with Scythrop is that he, like Flosky/Coleridge, has been taken in by the morbid self-indulgence and religiose delusion of German Romanticism:

> Scythrop was left alone at Nightmare Abbey. . . . The terrace terminated at the south-western tower, which, as we have said, was ruinous and full of owls. Here would Scythrop take his evening seat, on a fallen fragment of mossy stone . . . the Sorrows of Werter in his hand. . . . He began to devour romances and German tragedies, and, by the recommendation of Mr Flosky, to pore over ponderous tomes of transcendental

philosophy, which reconciled him to the labour of studying
them by their mystical jargon and necromantic imagery. In the
congenial solitude of Nightmare Abbey, the distempered ideas
of metaphysical romance and romantic metaphysics had ample
time and space to germinate into a fertile crop of chimeras. . . .
He passed whole mornings in his study, immersed in gloomy
reverie, stalking about the room in his nightcap, which he
pulled over his eyes like a cowl, and folding his striped calico
dressing-gown about him like the mantle of a conspirator.

(Garnett 1948: 362–63)

Any jibe about 'necromantic imagery' and 'gloomy reverie' was
mainly, of course, a jibe against the adolescent Shelley and the
Shelley of 1819 took the jest in good nature: 'I think Scythrop a
character admirably conceived and executed', he wrote to Peacock
(Ingpen and Peck 1965: X. 58). In his late teens Shelley had
published a number of Gothic novelettes and poems: *Zastrozzi*
(1810), *Original Poetry by Victor and Cazire* (with his sister
Elizabeth, 1810), and *St Irvyne or The Rosicrucian* (1811). Shelley
himself had tried to establish some distance from these productions as early as 1812 in his second letter to his future father-in-law
William Godwin. In this letter Shelley modified facts a little when
he stated that both *Zastrozzi* and *St Irvyne* were published
before he was 17, but the import of the letter, that the immature
phase of his indulgence in romance was over and that since
reading Godwin's *Political Justice* he had embarked upon a rational,
atheistical approach to problems of the real world, is clear enough:

From a reader, I became a writer of romances; before the age
of seventeen I had published two, 'St Irvyne' and 'Zastrozzi',
each of which, though quite uncharacteristic of me as now
I am, yet serves to mark the state of my mind at the period of
their composition. . . .

It is now a period of more than two years since first I saw
your inestimable book on 'Political Justice'; it opened to my

> mind fresh and more extensive views. . . . I was no longer the votary of romance; till then I had existed in an ideal world – now I found that in this universe of ours was enough to excite the interest of the heart, enough to employ the discussions of reason; I beheld, in short, that I had duties to perform. . . .
>
> I became, in the popular sense of the word 'God', an Atheist.
> . . .
>
> I am now. . . . writing 'An inquiry into the causes of the failure of the French Revolution to benefit mankind'. My plan is that of resolving to lose no opportunity to disseminate truth and happiness.
>
> (Ingpen and Peck 1965: VIII. 239–41)

Shelley's reading had not been restricted to the writings of Godwin. With his Oxford friend T.J. Hogg he had read the works of radicals, rationalists and sceptics like David Hume and Voltaire, Paine and Rousseau (Holmes 1976: 43). This immersion in enlightened thought lay behind Shelley's production in Dublin in 1812 of a pamphlet advocating Catholic emancipation and the repeal of the union with England, *An Address to the Irish People*, of which Richard Holmes has commented: 'This was the language of the nineties once more . . . the language of the French Revolutionary Convention, of Painites . . . of radical republicans' (Holmes 1976: 122). A comparable tone is struck in Shelley's 'Notes' on his poem *Queen Mab* (1813), of which Angela Leighton has commented: 'The long and fervent "Notes on Queen Mab" . . . bear witness to the sheer breadth of reading which fed Shelley's youthful radicalism, and helped him formulate a theory of social revolution inspired mainly by Enlightenment philosophes, English empiricists and Godwin' (Leighton 1984: 26–27). In these 'Notes' we find Shelley asserting:

> There is no real wealth but the labour of man. . . . In consequence of our consideration for the precious metals, one man is enabled to heap to himself luxuries at the expense of

the necessaries of his neighbour; a system admirably fitted to produce all the varieties of disease and crime, which never fail to characterize the two extremes of opulence and penury. . . .

The poor are set labour, – for what? Not the food for which they famish: not the blankets for want of which their babes are frozen by the cold of their miserable hovels . . . – no; for the pride of power, for the miserable isolation of pride, for the false pleasures of the hundredth part of society. . . .

I will not insult common sense by insisting on the doctrine of the natural equality of man. The question is not concerning its desirableness, but its practicability: so far as it is practicable, it is desirable. That state of human society which approaches nearer to an equal partition of its benefits and evils should, *caeteris paribus*, be preferred: but so long as we conceive that a wanton expenditure of human labour, not for the necessities, not even for the luxuries of the mass of society, but for the egotism and ostentation of a few of its members, is defensible on the ground of public justice, so long we neglect to approximate to the redemption of the human race.

(Hutchinson 1968: 804–805)

Shelley's concern for the famished poor, his commitment to 'the natural equality of man', influences his study of the solitary imagination in his 1816 poem 'Alastor; or the Spirit of Solitude'. This treats the search by a young poet for sublimity and perfection. He seems to find these in his own soul, figured in the poem by his dream of a 'veilèd maid':

A vision on his sleep
There came, a dream of hopes that never yet
Had flushed his cheek. He dreamed a veilèd maid
Sate near him, talking in low solemn tones.
Her voice was like the voice of his own soul
Heard in the calm of thought.

(149–54; Hutchinson 1968: 18)

When the poet wakes, the 'veiled maid' has vanished and the poem traces the poet's quest for her. But this quest for the ideal is a maddening one:

>                   He eagerly pursues
> Beyond the realms of dream that fleeting shade;
> He overleaps the bounds. Alas! Alas!
> Were limbs, and breath, and being intertwined
> Thus treacherously? Lost, lost, for ever lost,
> In the wide pathless desert of dim sleep,
> That beautiful shape! Does the dark gate of death
> Conduct to thy mysterious paradise,
> O sleep? . . .
> This doubt with sudden tide flowed on his heart,
> The insatiate hope which it awakened, stung
> His brain even like despair.
>                      While daylight held
> The sky, the Poet kept mute conference
> With his still soul. At night the passion came,
> Like the fierce fiend of a distempered dream,
> And shook him from his rest, and led him forth
> Into the darkness.
>
>       (205–13, 220–27; Hutchinson 1968: 19–20)

The poet in 'Alastor' pursues his vision beyond life itself. The problem is that the poem implies that the protagonist–poet's death may not be a consummation, may not be an achievement of spiritual fulness, but rather may be a demonstration of the solipsistic emptiness of an inward-looking spiritual orientation. The 'fierce fiend' in Shelley's study of narcissism contrasts with Wordsworth's self-solemnization in *The Prelude*:

>               to my soul I say
> "I recognise thy glory" . . .
>                 . . . in such visitings
> Of awful promise, when the light of sense

> Goes out in flashes that have shewn to us
> The invisible world.

> (1805, VI. 531–36; Wordsworth, Abrams and Gill 1979: 216)

'Alastor' may be read as a negative critique of the self-referential, self-mystifying, self-transcendentalizing Romantic ideology advanced by the mature Wordsworth or Coleridge. The protagonist–poet of 'Alastor', in his extreme introversion, makes the mistake of neglecting the human race. As Shelley puts it in his Preface to 'Alastor':

> The Poet's self-centred seclusion was avenged by the furies of an irresistible passion pursuing him to speedy ruin. . . . Among those who attempt to exist without human sympathy, the pure and tender-hearted perish through the intensity and passion of their search after its communities, when the vacancy of their spirit suddenly makes itself felt. All else. . . . who love not their fellow-beings live unfruitful lives, and prepare for their old age a miserable grave.

> (Hutchinson 1968: 15)

Shelley was not persuaded, as was Wordsworth, of the possibility of a meaningful relation between earthly existence and the invisible world. In 'Mont Blanc' (1817), instead of Wordsworth's or Coleridge's confidence in the providential nature of absolute power, we hear that

> Power dwells apart in its tranquillity,
> Remote, serene, and inaccessible:
> And *this*, the naked countenance of earth,
> On which I gaze, even these primaeval mountains
> Teach the adverting mind.

> (96–100; Hutchinson 1968: 534)

What teaches the mind is not a deified nature but a more empirically, scientifically apprehended nature. Attempting to 'exist without human sympathy' in private contemplation of spirit will lead only to a discovery of personal spiritual vacancy and of the sheer inaccessibility of absolute spirit or power. Shelley's is in many respects a secularized universe. It was precisely his lack of belief in some benevolent absolute power that led him to criticize those who insisted on individual communion with such a power and to emphasize, instead, the need for human beings to help each other here and now, on this earth.

A comparable point about the egocentric, anti-social tendencies of Romanticism was made by Mary Shelley in her novel *Frankenstein* (1818). *Frankenstein* pushes the Romantic model of the solitary, creative imagination to its extreme and illustrates its dangerous and destructive propensities. Driven by his voracious desire to pursue nature 'to her hiding-places' (Hindle 1985: 98), Frankenstein becomes neglectful of his friends and family:

> the same feelings which made me neglect the scenes around me caused me also to forget those friends who were so many miles absent, and whom I had not seen for so long a time. . . . but I could not tear my thoughts from my employment, loathsome in itself, but which had taken an irresistible hold of my imagination. I wished, as it were, to procrastinate all that related to my feelings of affection until the great object, which swallowed up every habit of my nature, should be completed.
>
> (Hindle 1985: 98–99)

The moment Frankenstein achieves his object, the creation of life from inanimate matter, the attractiveness of the quest evaporates: 'now that I had finished, the beauty of the dream vanished, and breathless horror and disgust filled my heart' (Hindle 1985: 101). Having abandoned social responsibilities in his quest, the further mistake Frankenstein makes is not to love the creature he has made. The Monster in Frankenstein is evil only because he is rejected by his creator and spurned by other human beings who see him. The real monster in *Frankenstein* is, of course, the creator of the Monster, Frankenstein himself. Egotism and selfishness breed evil. In the figure of the Monster *Frankenstein* literalizes or objectifies the destructiveness of the ego that would deny the importance of loving and generous social relationships. There is also a connection between Mary Shelley's representation of unregulated imagination and her representation of nature. The landscapes in the tenth chapter of the novel are icy, barren and inhospitable, as alien to warm humanity as Frankenstein's manic desire. In her description of mountains in this chapter Mary Shelley invokes Romantic treatments of the sublime as that which exceeds formulation and representation, that which signifies transcendence. And she places Frankenstein's Monster – as the grotesque objectification of the self's own sublime potential – within this awesome, typically Romantic landscape. Instead of being celebrated, however, the more-than-human, the sublime, is here portrayed as inimical to the human, as dangerously inhuman:

> The field of ice is almost a league in width, but I spent nearly two hours in crossing it. . . . From the side where I now stood Montanvert was exactly opposite . . . and above it rose Mont Blanc, in awful majesty. I remained in a recess of the rock, gazing on this wonderful and stupendous scene. . . .
>
> I suddenly beheld the figure of a man, at some distance, advancing towards me with superhuman speed. He bounded over the crevices in the ice, among which I had walked with caution; his stature, also, as he approached, seemed to exceed that of man. I was troubled. . . . I perceived, as the shape came nearer (sight tremendous and abhorred!) that it was the wretch whom I had created. . . .
>
> He . . . said. . . . 'Believe me, Frankenstein, I was benevolent; my soul glowed with love and humanity; but am I not alone, miserably alone? You, my creator, abhor me; what hope can I gather from your fellow creatures, who owe me nothing? They spurn and hate me. The desert mountains and dreary glaciers

are my refuge. . . . These bleak skies I hail, for they are kinder to me than your fellow beings. If the multitude of mankind knew of my existence, they would do as you do, and arm themselves for my destruction. Shall I not then hate them who abhor me?'

(Hindle 1985: 140–42)

Mary Shelley's is an analysis, parallelling Percy Shelley's in 'Alastor', of the destructiveness of that cult of the individual, that cult of solitariness and introversion, which grew up in the wake of the failure of early, idealist hopes for social renovation. Percy Shelley's opposition to that cult emerges again in *The Revolt of Islam*, which was first published as *Laon and Cythna* late in 1817 and republished under its new title in 1818. In his Preface to *The Revolt of Islam* Shelley observed:

The sympathies connected with that event [the French Revolution] extended to every bosom. . . . But such a degree of unmingled good was expected as it was impossible to realize. . . . The revulsion occasioned by the atrocities of the demagogues and the re-establishment of successive tyrannies in France, was terrible. . . . many of the most ardent and tender-hearted of the worshippers of public good have been morally ruined by what a partial glimpse of the events they deplored appeared to show as the melancholy desolation of all their cherished hopes. Hence gloom and misanthropy have become the characteristics of the age in which we live, the solace of a disappointment that unconsciously finds relief only in the wilful exaggeration of its own despair. This influence has tainted the literature of the age with the hopelessness of the minds from which it flows. Metaphysics, and inquiries into moral and political science, have become little else than vain attempts to revive exploded superstitions . . . calculated to lull the oppressors of mankind into a security of everlasting triumph. Our works of fiction and poetry have been over-shadowed by the same infectious gloom. But mankind appear to me to be emerging from their trance.

> I am aware, methinks, of a slow, gradual, silent change. In that
> belief I have composed the following Poem.
>
> > (Hutchinson 1968: 33–34)

*The Revolt of Islam* is set in Greece and it offers a vision of human
hope and love surviving the depths of wintry oppression. Towards
the end of Canto IX the freedom-fighter Laon foresees his own and
Cythna's deaths but still declares that freedom will reassert itself
with the gradual, inevitable momentum of a natural force:

> The seeds are sleeping in the soil: meanwhile
> > The Tyrant peoples dungeons with his prey,
> Pale victims on the guarded scaffold smile
> > Because they cannot speak; and, day by day,
> > The moon of wasting Science wanes away
> Among her stars, and in that darkness vast
> > The sons of earth to their vast idols pray,
> And gray Priests triumph, and like blight or blast
> A shade of selfish care o'er human looks is cast.
>
> This is the winter of the world; – and here
> > We die, even as the winds of Autumn fade,
> Expiring in the frore and foggy air. –
> > Behold! Spring comes, though we must pass, who made
> > The promise of its birth, – even as the shade
> Which from our death, as from a mountain, flings
> > The future, a broad sunrise; thus arrayed
> As with the plumes of overshadowing wings,
> From its dark gulf of chains, Earth like an eagle springs.
> > (!X. xxiv–xxv. 3676–93; Hutchinson 1968: 127–28)

Shelley remained true to the Enlightenment inheritance of
political radicalism throughout his poetry following *The Revolt of
Islam*. The use of classical subjects as a means of exploring this
radicalism also formed a consistent strain in Shelley's work and

this sympathy with specifically Hellenic poetry and philosophy, as against the Roman Augustan classics, may be seen as symptomatic of Shelley's perpetuation of Enlightenment tastes. From *Prometheus Unbound* (1820), Shelley's symbolic account of the overthrow of tyranny, to *Hellas* (1822), published in the year he died, Shelley offered his own versions of Enlightenment values. As Richard Holmes has written:

> The myth of Prometheus the fire-bringer and liberator of mankind was already a familiar force in the liberal culture of the nineteenth century. . . . Politically the myth of Prometheus had always been present in the 'progressive philosophy' of rationality and revolution which had swept over Europe since the date of Shelley's own birth. The French Revolutionaries had been Promethean by adoption. . . . [*Hellas*] contrasts . . . the difference between the great rational and humane tradition of classical Greek philosophy, with the superseding ideology of guilt and punishment represented for Shelley by the supreme authoritarianism of institutionalized Christian religion. . . . altogether the work represents one of the most sophisticated and historically mature statements of Shelley's atheism. . . . the drama is rightly celebrated for its declaration of Philhellenism.
>
> (Holmes 1976: 490–91, 678)

Just as Shelley moved from Gothic romance in *Zastrozzi* to the Hellenism of *Hellas*, so Byron moved from an infatuation with German-style gloom in poems like *Childe Harold's Pilgrimage*, to the lighter, comic, rationalist-sceptical mode of his unfinished classic *Don Juan* (1819–24). The narrative in *Don Juan* is not the structural principle of the poem. That lies with the personality and perspectives of the narrator. The poem is a monologue in which the narrator tells a picaresque story of the life and adventures of Don Juan. The Don Juan of tradition was the Spanish libertine with notable sexual proclivities. An unstated joke of Byron's poem is that while Don Juan does have numerous romantic encounters, he is not the calculating initiator of these encounters, but the object of the women who pursue him. The narrative voice of *Don Juan* goes on for nearly two thousand stanzas telling us Don Juan's story while using the occasions of that story to confide in us his opinions and judgements of the institutions and values of contemporary European society.

Byron wrote a 'Dedication' to *Don Juan* in 1818. This was not published with the first two cantos of the poem in 1819 since it was thought by his publisher and friends too extreme in its attacks on Castlereagh (1769–1822), Britain's enormously powerful Foreign Secretary from 1812 to 1822. Byron objected vehemently to Castlereagh's policy of sustaining reactionary monarchies throughout Europe and termed him an 'intellectual eunuch' (I. xi. 8; Page 1970: 636). In *The Vision of Judgement*, published in 1822, Byron attacked George III and Robert Southey. *The Vision of Judgement* was provoked by Southey's poem of 1821, *A Vision of Judgement*, which had contained a eulogy of George III. In *The Vision of Judgement* George III, who died in 1820, is characterized as one who 'ever warr'd with freedom and the free:/ . . . /So that they utter'd the word "Liberty!"/Found George the Third their first opponent' (XLV. 1, 3–4; Page 1970: 162).

'The New World shook him off; the Old yet groans
  Beneath what he and his prepared, if not
Completed: he leaves his heirs on many thrones
  To all his vices.'

(XLVII. 1–4; Page 1970: 162)

These words are spoken by Satan who is arguing against the dead George III being allowed to enter Paradise. The celestial debate on this matter is interrupted by Robert Southey who drives everyone crazy with a boring and conceited speech. While Southey is droning on George III slips quietly into Paradise.

Moreover, in the 'Dedication' to *Don Juan* Byron links his

attacks on Castlereagh with what he saw as the obscure and frequently reactionary attitudes of the Lake poets, Southey, Wordsworth and Coleridge:

> Bob Southey! You're a poet – Poet-laureate,
>   And representative of all the race;
> Although 'tis true that you turn'd out a Tory at
>   Last, – yours has lately been a common case;
> And now, my Epic Renegade! what are ye at?
>   With all the Lakers, in and out of place? . . .
>
>
> . . . Coleridge, too, has lately taken wing,
>   But like a hawk encumber'd with his hood, –
> Explaining metaphysics to the nation –
> I wish he would explain his Explanation . . .
>
>
> And Wordsworth, in a rather long 'Excursion'
>   (I think the quarto holds five hundred pages),
> Has given a sample from the vasty version
>   Of his new system to perplex the sages . . .
>
> (i. 1–6, ii. 5–8, iv. 1–4; Page 1970: 635)

In the course of *Don Juan* itself Byron continues his humorous assault on what he saw as the pretensions of the mature Wordsworth and Coleridge, with their idealizations of the self and the cosmos:

> Young Juan wander'd by the glassy brooks,
>   Thinking unutterable things; he threw
> Himself at length within the leafy nooks
>   Where the wild branch of the cork forest grew;
> There poets find materials for their books,
>   And every now and then we read them through,
> So that their plan and prosody are eligible,
> Unless, like Wordsworth, they prove unintelligible.

He, Juan (and not Wordsworth), so pursued
  His self-communion with his own high soul,
Until his mighty heart, in its great mood,
  Had mitigated part, though not the whole
Of its disease; he did the best he could
  With things not very subject to control,
And turn'd, without perceiving his condition,
Like Coleridge, into a metaphysician.

He thought about himself, and the whole earth,
  Of man the wonderful, and of the stars,
And how the deuce they ever could have birth;
  And then he thought of earthquakes, and of wars,
How many miles the moon might have in girth,
  Of air-balloons, and of the many bars
To perfect knowledge of the boundless skies; –
And then he thought of Donna Julia's eyes.

In thoughts like these true wisdom may discern
  Longings sublime, and aspirations high,
Which some are born with, but the most part learn
  To plague themselves withal, they know not why:
'Twas strange that one so young should thus concern
  His brain about the action of the sky;
If *you* think 'twas philosophy that this did,
I can't help thinking puberty assisted.

(I. xc–xciii; Page 1970: 647)

Byron had been anticipated in such debunking of idealist pre-
tension, perceptively if less brilliantly, by the Scottish writer James
Hogg (1770–1835). In 1816 Hogg published, in *The Poetic
Mirror*, a poem entitled 'James Rigg', which was headed as a 'Still
Further Extract from *The Recluse, A Poem*'. The following passage
from 'James Rigg', which deals with the opening of a door to a

house, parodies Wordsworth's manner of finding eternal significance in the most mundane of actions and objects:

> th' obedient door,
> As at a potent necromancer's touch,
> Into the air receded suddenly,
> And gave wide prospect of the sparkling lake,
> Just then emerging from the snow-white mist
> Like angel's veil slow-folded up to heaven.
> And lo! a vision bright and beautiful
> Sheds a refulgent glory o'er the sand,
> The sand and gravel of my avenue!

(10–18; Mack 1970: 62)

The political radicalism which motivates the sceptical comedy of Byron's *Don Juan* shows the poet to be calling on a tradition of thought which predated his own earlier indulgence in introverted posturing, his own earlier creation of guilt-ridden, angst-ridden heroes. Angus Calder has summarized the nature of Byron's reaction against the cult of the individual spirit:

Byron, like his friend Shelley and Shelley's friend Peacock, was a writer aligned with radicalism through harking back to the eighteenth-century Enlightenment, with its pronounced tendency to reject Christianity. . . . Why did 'bourgeois' thought deify the poet's 'individual genius' while accepting, and even *enforcing*, his separateness from society? Why did the (surely pernicious) myth arise that poetry has nothing to do with everyday life, but is holy and apart? . . .

To the Adam Smith-ite or Bentham-ite reformer, everything which was not 'useful' ('use' being defined in economic terms) must be excluded from the sphere in which commerce, manufacture and statecraft worked out their 'progressive' destinies. Literature was acceptable *only* as a 'serious' recreation, as a necessary safety-valve for feelings and imaginings which might otherwise interfere with business. Meanwhile, the Evangelical or Tory Churchman could accept poetry only as a handmaid to 'pure', that is to 'religious', feeling. Wordsworth's poetry was increasingly acceptable because it derived from a kind of religious experience in an area, 'the Lakes', which was remote from the more blatant manifestations of industrialization, and thus easy to mystify.

Don Juan was directed, by an on-the-whole repentant 'Byronist', against the whole 'bourgeois' ideological cluster in which the Toryism of Castlereagh overlapped with aspects of 'Laker' religious feeling, with Evangelicalism, and with the interests of manufacturers in controlling the pleasures of the poor.

(Calder 1987: 67, 69)

John Keats, too, in his particularly short career as a poet, shows something of a move from an early concern with an interior, spiritual world towards an increasing awareness of the drawbacks of such interiority and towards an engagement with external realities. The story of *Endymion* (1818), written when Keats was eighteen, is based on the classical myth of the love between a mortal and the goddess of the moon. It tells of Endymion's search for a divine being whom he has seen in visions. In the course of his search he meets and falls in love with an Indian maid, in apparent contradiction of his search for the divine ideal. But there is, in fact, no real contradiction since the Indian maid turns out to be Cynthia or Diana, goddess of the moon and the divine being of his earlier visions. The moon goddess or Indian maid stands to Endymion much as the 'veilèd maid' stands to the poet–protagonist in Shelley's 'Alastor'. She is an anima figure, an objectification of a dimension of Endymion's own self. Hence there are narcissistic connotations in some of his early visions of the divine maid: 'A wonder, fair as any I have told – /The same bright face I tasted in my sleep,/Smiling in the clear well' (I. 894–96; Allott 1970: 159–60).

But unlike Shelley's treatment of self-referentiality in 'Alastor', where the poet–protagonist may be lost in a solipsistic void, in Keats's *Endymion* the hero ends up finding his desired ideal embodied in the Indian maid and from his 'mortal state' he is somehow 'spiritualized' (IV. 991, 993; Allott 1970: 284). It is, of course, a big somehow. The exact nature of the relations between the mortal realm and the infinite or the ideal are never specified. 'Wherein lies happiness?', asks Endymion in the first canto of the poem, and he goes on to assert what the poem as a whole asserts:

Wherein lies happiness? In that which becks
Our ready minds to fellowship divine,
A fellowship with essence, till we shine
Full alchemized, and free of space. Behold
The clear religion of heaven!

(I. 777–81; Allott 1970: 154)

But this is all assertion and not demonstration. *Endymion* is an almost absurdly idealistic fantasy which wishes to reconcile and harmonize the earthly and the unearthly without ever showing the grounds of such reconciliation.

Keats began very shortly to start qualifying and asking questions about the kind of high Romantic idealism evident in *Endymion*. In 'Ode to a Nightingale' (1819), for example, the nightingale itself, which 'Singest of summer in full-throated ease' (10; Allott 1970: 525), can be read as an emblem of poetic expression and ideal artistic achievement. The speaker of the poem first imagines getting drunk and so leaving the world and joining the nightingale: 'Oh, for a beaker full of the warm South . . . /That I might drink, and leave the world unseen,/And with thee fade away into the forest dim' (15, 19–20; Allott 1970: 526). He then imagines joining the nightingale 'charioted' not 'by Bacchus' but 'on the viewless wings of Poesy' (32–33; Allott 1970: 527). Poetry, together with the nightingale's song that emblematizes poetry, is associated with something rich and magical that transcends individual life and indeed history itself:

> No hungry generations tread thee down;
> The voice I heard this passing night was heard
> In ancient days by emperor and clown . . .
> The same that oft-times hath
> Charmed magic casements. . .

(62–64, 68–69; Allott 1970: 530)

But this eulogy of the life of the imagination is actually unstable. Keats continues:

> Charmed magic casements, opening on the foam
> Of perilous seas in fairy lands forlorn.

(69–70; Allott 1970: 530)

This might appear an endorsement of wonderfully tense imaginative adventures in some remote ('forlorn') past. But the peril and the woebegoneness ('forlorn') touch an anxiety that runs throughout the poem. This is that imaginative adventure, indulgence in poetry itself, may be a culpable evasion of the real world. Earlier in the poem the speaker has fancied that, following the nightingale, he will 'Fade far away, dissolve, and quite forget' (21; Allott 1970: 526) what the nightingale has never known:

> The weariness, the fever, and the fret
> Here, where men sit and hear each other groan;
> Where palsy shakes a few, sad, last gray hairs,
> Where youth grows pale, and spectre-thin, and dies;
> Where but to think is to be full of sorrow . . .

(23–27; Allott 1970: 526–27)

The kind of imaginative reverie associated with the nightingale's song is, in other words, an escape from the actual world. The last stanza of 'Ode to a Nightingale' is shot through with uncertainty about the relation between the real and the ideal or imaginative.

The speaker is here returned from absorption in the realm defined by the nightingale to his ordinary self. The 'fancy' is not as successful in transfiguring the real as is sometimes supposed. Indeed, the imaginative transfiguration of the real may be no more than a cheat, a deception. The nightingale's song recedes and the speaker is uncertain whether to associate that song with genuine vision or merely with the illusoriness of a dream. At the very end of the final stanza it is not clear to the speaker whether the loss of the song means that he has woken to the common sense of common experience or whether such waking is, in fact, a kind of dormancy which closes off access to imaginative vision. At any rate, reconciling worldly and ideal realms is not as easy as was envisaged in *Endymion*:

> Forlorn! The very word is like a bell
>   To toll me back from thee to my sole self!
> Adieu! The fancy cannot cheat so well
>   As she is famed to do, deceiving elf.
> Adieu! adieu! Thy plaintive anthem fades
>   Past the near meadows, over the still stream,
>     Up the hill-side; and now 'tis buried deep
>       In the next valley-glades:
>   Was it a vision, or a waking dream?
>     Fled is that music . . . Do I wake or sleep?
>
> (71–80; Allott 1970: 531–32)

These kinds of questions about the relations between poetic vision and the real world preoccupied Keats very much in the few years before his death in 1821. There is evidence in his letters that he was beginning to define for himself a position of social commitment that stood in clear contrast with the idea of an imaginative and spiritual retreat from society. In a letter written between 17 and 27 September 1819 we find him observing:

> All civilized countries become gradually more enlighten'd. . . .
> in every Kingdom there was a long struggle of Kings to destroy

all popular privileges. . . . The example of England, and the liberal writers of france and england sowed the seed of opposition to this Tyranny – and it was swelling in the ground till it burst out in the french revolution. That has had an unlucky termination. It put a stop to the rapid progress of free sentiments in England; and gave our Court hopes of turning back to the despotism of the 16 century. They have made a handle of this event in every way to undermine our freedom. They spread a horrid superstition against all innovation and improvement. The present struggle in England of the people is to destroy this superstition. . . . This is no contest between whig and tory – but between right and wrong.

(Forman 1952: 406–407)

## ROMANTICISM AND CONSERVATISM

'All civilized countries become gradually more enlighten'd'. Turning now to address the title of this chapter, 'Enlightenment *and* Romantic', I want to recapitulate some elements of the argument of this book so far. In respect of Wordsworth, Coleridge, Blake and Southey, I have suggested that their earlier work, showing distinct political radicalism, may be described as late Enlightenment in nature. The radicalism in that earlier work chimes with the radicalism of other creative writers in the 1780s and 1790s, such as Helen Maria Williams, Robert Burns, Charlotte Smith, or the contributors to magazines and journals whose writings have been summarized by Robert Mayo. It chimes with, or is the literary corollary of, Enlightenment treatises such as Paine's *Rights of Man*. But Wordsworth, Coleridge and Southey came to change their minds over the issue of radicalism once the French Revolution had disappointed early hopes. Even Blake retreated into 'an effectively depoliticized' private mythology (Butler 1981: 51). The 'great' works of a figure like Wordsworth – including the 'Immortality Ode', *The Prelude*, and *The Excursion* – can be seen to stand for a socio-political position which is the opposite of revolutionary. Wordsworth's and, for that matter, Coleridge's later emphasis on spiritual matters, on the ultimate value of the individual imagination, is something which squares not with political radicalism but rather with political conservatism, either explicit or implicit. The emphasis on interiority may be seen as part of a reactionary, counter-revolutionary impulse. In this emphasis on interiority and spirituality the British writers have a great deal in common with the Germans who first established the term 'Romantic' in its more modern sense. German Romanticism, as I have noted, tended to be a counter-revolutionary movement. So if it is appropriate to typify the early work of the British writers as late Enlightenment in character, then it is equally appropriate to typify their mature work as Romantic, so long as it is understood that the term Romantic is not to be associated with the politically radical.

When M.H. Abrams spoke of Wordsworth effecting in his poetry 'an egalitarian revolution of the spirit' (quoted p. 100) he was repeating that approval of the transcendental displacement of socio-political energy which was characteristic of much commentary on the Romantics in the nineteenth century – commentary exemplified by Edward Dowden's 1897 *The French Revolution and English Literature*. As well as questionably associating the mature works of the first generation of British Romantics with a principle of revolution, such identifications avoid mentioning that, as well as confident spiritualization, there was another kind of response to the failure of Enlightenment social idealism. This was a response of introverted gloom and despair. Gloom at the loss of social hope, no doubt, but also a despairing loss of confidence in those inner resources of the self which were supposed to sustain the individual who has lost social hope. Such darker feelings are not really allowed in Abrams' definition of Romanticism. As Jerome McGann has written:

> Abrams' deeply influential ideas are clearly drawn from a
> Wordsworthian and, more generally, a Christian (Protestant)

model. . . . these ideas . . . propose a moral evaluation of the 'message' of 'the great Romantic poems' as well as a certain canonization of the phenomena. 'Despair' is an emotional state to be shunned if not deplored, and it is associated explicitly with 'the unbounded and hence impossible hopes' of political and social transformation. 'Hope', on the other hand, is a good thing, and it is associated with an 'infinite *Sehnsucht*' which is possible to achieve: that is, with a psychological victory, a religious and spiritual success which can replace the failed hope of social melioration.

[Abrams'] Romantic world . . . is . . . a good and happy place: a place of enthusiasm, creative process, celebration, and something evermore about to be.

(McGann 1983: 26–27)

Such a world has no place for the alienated self-indulgence of Byron's *Childe Harold's Pilgrimage*, the anxieties about the efficacy of the imagination in Keats' *Odes*; it has no accounting for poems like Coleridge's 'Phantom or Fact' (1834), John Clare's (1793–1864) 'Sonnet: I Am' (written after 1842), Wordsworth's 'Elegiac Stanzas' (1807), or George Crabbe's 'Peter Grimes' (1810).

Coleridge's 'Phantom or Fact. A Dialogue in Verse' manifests a serious dubiety about the idealization of self that was a Romantic staple:

### Author

A lovely form there sate beside my bed,
And such a feeding calm its presence shed,
A tender love so pure from earthly leaven,
That I unnethe the fancy might control,
'Twas my own spirit newly come from heaven,
Wooing its gentle way into my soul!
But ah! the change – It had not stirr'd, and yet –
Alas! that change how fain would I forget!
That shrinking back, like one that had mistook!

That weary, wandering, disavowing look!
'Twas all another, feature, look, and frame,
And still, methought, I knew, it was the same!

*Friend*

This riddling tale, to what does it belong?
Is't history? vision? or an idle song?
Or rather say at once, within what space
Of time this wild disastrous change took place?

*Author*

Call it a moment's work (and such it seems)
This tale's a fragment from the life of dreams;
But say, that years matur'd the silent strife,
And 'tis a record from the dream of life.

(Coleridge 1912: I. 404–405)

Comparable to this poem is John Clare's 'Sonnet: I Am', which also records a loss of sustaining Romantic myths about the self:

I feel I am; – I only know I am,
And plod upon the earth, as dull and void:
Earth's prison chilled my body with its dram
Of dullness, and my soaring thoughts destroyed,
I fled to solitudes from passions dream,
But strife pursued – I only know, I am,
I was a being created in the race
Of men disdaining bounds of place and time: –
A spirit that could travel o'er the space
Of earth and heaven, – like a thought sublime,
Tracing creation, like my maker, free, –
A soul unshackled – like eternity,
Spurning earth's vain and soul debasing thrall
But now I only know I am, – that's all.

(Robinson and Powell 1984: I. 397–98)

In Wordsworth's 'Elegaic Stanzas: Suggested by a Picture of Peele Castle, In a Storm, Painted by Sir George Beaumont', the poet tells how in the past, if he had been the painter, he would have represented Peele Castle as a token of his faith in a benevolent universe:

> I would have planted thee, thou hoary Pile!
> Amid a world how different from this!
> Beside a sea that could not cease to smile;
> On tranquil land, beneath a sky of bliss.
>
> . . .
>
> A Picture had it been of lasting ease,
> Elysian quiet, without toil or strife;
> No motion but the moving tide, a breeze,
> Or merely silent Nature's breathing life.
>
> Such, in the fond delusion of my heart,
> Such Picture would I at that time have made:
> And seen the soul of truth in every part;
> A faith, a trust, that could not be betrayed.
>
> (17–20, 25–32; Gill 1984: 326–27)

But in this poem that faith in the fundamentally positive character of 'silent Nature's breathing life' *has* been betrayed: 'So once it would have been, – 'tis so no more;/I have submitted to a new controul:/A power is gone, which nothing can restore' (33–35; Gill 1984: 327). The loss of the old apprehension of power within and without leads Wordsworth to an uncharacteristic vision of a violent and threatening natural world bereft of saving spiritual grace:

> Then Beaumont . . .
> This Work of thine I blame not, but commend;
> This sea in anger, and the dismal shore.
>
> Oh 'tis a passionate Work! – yet wise and well;
> Well chosen is the spirit that is here;

> That Hulk which labours in the deadly swell,
> This rueful sky, this pageantry of fear!

> And this huge Castle, standing here sublime,
> I love to see the look with which it braves,
> Cased in the unfeeling armour of old time,
> The light'ning, the fierce wind, and trampling waves.
>
> (41, 43–52; Gill 1984: 327)

A comparably dark vision, though of a subtly different kind, controls George Crabbe's (1754–1832) presentation of his protagonist in 'Peter Grimes', which was one of the tales of *The Borough* (1810). Crabbe never held a high Romantic idealism about the human mind, but his interest in the negative potentialities of the mind contrasts sharply with such idealism. 'Peter Grimes' tells the story of a poor fisherman who maltreats and causes the deaths of three 'Parish-Boys' (62; Dalrymple-Champneys and Pollard 1988: I. 566), orphans who have been indentured to him as labourers or work-helps. The poem tells of Grimes' later hallucinations, apparently generated by guilt. But the work does not hold out the possibility of Grimes' redemption through repentance. It merely ends with his tortured delirious visions of the spirits of the three dead boys as well as of his dead father, whom he had abused years before. What is interesting about the poem is that it leaves obscure the sources of Peter Grimes' perverted mind. The presentation of Grimes is deeply interior but bereft of any idealist transfiguration of the subjective. Here, going within the mind means to enter a realm of ultimately inexplicable malignancy. Crabbe uses nature to image the disturbing and disturbed energies of mind, as in the following lines which describe Grimes after the death of the third boy:

> When Tides were neap, and, in the sultry day,
> Through the tall bounding Mud-banks made their way,
> Which on each side rose swelling, and below

The dark warm Flood ran silently and slow;
There anchoring, *Peter* chose from man to hide,
There hang his Head, and view the lazy Tide
In its hot slimy Channel slowly glide.

(181–87; Dalrymple-Champneys and Pollard 1988: 569–70)

The darker Romantic moods of poems such as Wordsworth's 'Elegiac Stanzas' or Coleridge's 'Phantom or Fact' lead Jerome McGann to sympathize with the arguments of an early twentieth-century commentator on Romanticism, Arthur O. Lovejoy. In an essay first published in 1924 Lovejoy argued against the idea that there was a single, monolithic phenomenon which could be called Romanticism. His essay, entitled 'On the Discrimination of Romanticisms', suggested that:

> we should learn to use the word 'Romanticism' in the plural. This, of course, is already the practise of the more cautious and observant literary historians, in so far as they recognise that the 'Romanticism' of one country may have little in common with that of another. . . . But the discrimination of Romanticisms which I have in mind is not solely or chiefly a division upon lines of nationality or language. What is needed is that any study of the subject should begin with a recognition of a *prima facie* plurality of Romanticisms, of possibly quite distinct thought-complexes, a number of which may appear in one country.

(Lovejoy 1924: 235–36)

The suggestion that we should speak of Romanticisms fits the argument of this book better than the idea that it is possible to speak of a single, self-consistent thing called Romanticism. Here I have suggested that the earlier, politically radical work of the first generation British 'Romantic' writers is better termed late Enlightenment. Their mature, conservative writings may be called Romantic, so long as Romantic is taken neither to signify political radicalism nor to mean simply the enthusiastic and celebratory, but may include the inverse of those states, a falling away from confidence in the imagination that is a product of previous over-intense trust in imagination.

When it comes to the second generation of writers, it is likewise possible to find in their work features which may be defined as Romantic and features which may be defined as late Enlighten-ment. The Romantic features may be either the confident idealism of, say, Keats' *Endymion* or the darker tones of, say, Byron's *Childe Harold's Pilgrimage*. The late Enlightenment would be represented by the political radicalism of Shelley's *The Revolt of Islam* and *Hellas*, or the radical scepticism of Byron's *Don Juan*. The most important item in such a way of defining the literary productions of late eighteenth and early nineteenth-century Britain is that, unlike the definitions in *The Oxford Companion to English Literature* or in Abrams' *Glossary of Literary Terms*, Romanticism is identified above all as being a politically conservative, sometimes reactionary tendency of thought and attitude. Equally the writings of those who have formerly been defined as Romantic are not necessarily anti-Enlightenment in any simple sense. The political radicalism which exists in the period, purveyed by supposedly 'Romantic' writers, is better seen as a late Enlightenment phenom-enon, whether it occurs in the 1790s or, as in the case of the younger 'Romantics', in the second two decades of the nineteenth century.

I want to conclude this book with a chapter on a further way of reading the 'Romantic' period of literature which has been gaining ground in the last decade or so. Studies in gender issues complement, complicate, and open out the period for yet further reconsideration.

# 4

## GENDER AND
## THE SUBLIME

In *A Philosophical Enquiry into the Origin of our Ideas of the Sublime and Beautiful* (1757) Edmund Burke, attempting to define the experience of the sublime, spoke of an experience of a power that exceeds the quantifiable and the usable. Encounters with such a power, he observed, are characterized by pain and terror rather than by pleasure and love. For sublime power so transcends the bounds of the finite and the mortal that the individual has the sense of being threatened with obliteration when encountering it. Experience of the sublime is thus marked by a terrifying thrill rather than by pleasurable affection:

> I know of nothing sublime which is not some modification of power. And this . . . rises . . . from terror, the common stock of every thing that is sublime. . . . pleasure follows the will; and therefore we are generally affected with it by many things of a force greatly inferior to our own. But pain is always inflicted by a power in some way superior, because we never submit to pain willingly. So that strength, violence, pain and terror, are

ideas that rush in upon the mind together. ... Whenever strength is only useful, and employed for our benefit or our pleasure, then it is never sublime; for nothing can act agreeably to us, that does not act in conformity to our will; but to act agreeably to our will, it must be subject to us; and therefore can never be the cause of a grand and commanding conception.

(Burke 1990: 59–61)

The grand and commanding conceptions produced by the sublime are not, of course, subject to rational disquisition. Burke says of the nature of the sublime:

The passion caused by the great and sublime in *nature* ... is Astonishment; and astonishment is that state of the soul, in which all its motions are suspended, with some degree of horror. In this case the mind is so entirely filled with its object, that it cannot entertain any other, nor by consequence reason on that object which employs it. Hence arises the great power of the sublime, that far from being produced by them, it anticipates our reasonings, and hurries us on by an irresistible force.

(Burke 1990: 53)

Burke found the sublime in anything earthly that could produce the impression of infinity: in natural phenomena and in human constructions whose dimensions, particularly along the vertical line, are huge and grand: in the overwhelming mass of mountains or in deep, dark caves, in soaring buildings, particularly ruins, or even in poetry (such as that in the Old Testament or in Homer) which celebrates the superhuman or the divine. Burke says of infinity:

Another source of the sublime, is *infinity*. ... Infinity has a tendency to fill the mind with that sort of delightful horror, which is the most genuine effect, and truest test of the sublime. There are scarce any things which can become the objects of our senses that are really, and in their own nature infinite. But the eye not being able to perceive the bounds of many things, they seem to be infinite, and they produce the same effects as if they were really so.

(Burke 1990: 67)

The ultimate sublime object is, of course, God:

when we contemplate the Deity, his attributes and their operation coming united on the mind, form a sort of sensible image, and as such are capable of affecting the imagination. . . . whilst we contemplate so vast an object, under the arm, as it were, of almighty power, and invested upon every side with omnipresence, we shrink into the minuteness of our own nature, and are, in a manner, annihilated before him. . . . If we rejoice, we rejoice with trembling.

(Burke 1990: 62–63)

The masculine gendering of the ultimate sublime object is, needless to say, no merely superficial convention. Burke defines the beautiful in contrast with the sublime and while, in his definition, the term beautiful may be applied to physical objects, to animals and to men as well as to women, the characteristics of this phenomenon, which is of a lesser order than the sublime, are what have conventionally been thought of as 'feminine' characteristics, such as softness, smallness, smoothness and delicacy. Unlike the awesome, divine, spiritual power of the sublime, beauty is envisaged as a merely sensory phenomenon, something involved in generating feelings of love, a passion which is 'directed to the multiplication of the species' (Burke 1990: 38). 'By beauty', Burke writes,

I mean, that quality or those qualities in bodies by which they cause love, or some passion similar to it. . . . There is a wide difference between admiration and love. The sublime, which is the cause of the former, always dwells on great objects, and terrible; the latter on small ones and pleasing.

(Burke 1990: 103)

'[S]trength', says Burke, which can be one of the qualities of the sublime, is 'very prejudicial to beauty. An appearance of *delicacy*, and even of fragility, is almost essential to it' (Burke 1990: 105). And this essentially 'feminine' characteristic is fused by Burke with actual women when he writes: '[T]he beauty of women is considerably owing to their weakness, or delicacy, and is even enhanced by their timidity, a quality of mind analogous to it' (Burke 1990: 106). A profoundly gendered economy controls Burke's definition of the sublime and the beautiful, where the major term, the sublime, is masculinized and the lesser term, the beautiful, is feminized. As Anne K. Mellor has observed:

> Burke's aesthetic classifications participated in, and helped to support, a powerful hegemonic sexual politics. As he constructed the category of the beautiful, Burke also constructed the image of the ideal woman, as his illustrative remarks reveal. Beauty is identified with the 'softer virtues' [Burke 1990: 100], with easiness of temper, compassion, kindness and liberality, as opposed to the higher qualities of mind, those virtues which cause admiration such as fortitude, justice and wisdom, and which Burke assigned to the masculine sublime. . . .
>
> Beauty, for Burke, is identified not only with the nurturing mother but also with the erotic love-object, the sensuous and possessible beloved. Identifying beauty with the small . . . Burke revealingly commented that 'we submit to what we admire, but we love what submits to us' [Burke 1990: 103]. The ideal woman, then, is one who engages in a practice of what today we would call female masochism, willingly obeying the dictates of her sublime master.
>
> (Mellor 1993: 108)

Burke's ideas on the sublime find a parallel, not an exact correspondence, in Wordsworth's celebration of his own imaginative apprehension of a power that transcends nature and the senses. In Book VI of *The Prelude*, where he describes his crossing of the

Alps, Wordsworth conflated his own 'Imagination' (1805, VI. 525; Wordsworth, Abrams and Gill 1979: 216) with an ultimate power when he spoke of 'visitings/Of awful promise, when the light of sense/Goes out in flashes that have shewn to us/The invisible world' (1805, VI. 533–36; Wordsworth, Abrams and Gill 1979: 216). A comparably sublime moment occurs again in Book XIII of *The Prelude*. Here Wordsworth describes intimations, gained during an ascent of Mount Snowdon, of 'The soul, the imagination of the whole' (1805, XIII. 65; Wordsworth, Abrams and Gill 1979: 460). In the Snowdon passage Wordsworth is again interested in something that transcends nature and the senses. Nature is important in that it does itself intimate this ultimate reality. Wordsworth describes how he breaks through a layer of mist in his ascent of Snowdon and suddenly finds everything illumined by the moon. He sees how the mist appears like a sea and how this mist-sea usurps the place of the real sea:

> instantly a light upon the turf
> Fell like a flash. I looked about, and lo,
> The moon stood naked in the heavens at height
> Immense above my head, and on the shore
> I found myself of a huge sea of mist,
> Which meek and silent rested at my feet.
> A hundred hills their dusky backs upheaved
> All over this still ocean, and beyond,
> Far, far beyond, the vapours shot themselves
> In headlands, tongues, and promontary shapes,
> Into the sea, the real sea, that seemed
> To dwindle and give up its majesty,
> Usurped upon as far as sight could reach.

> (1805, XIII. 39–51; Wordsworth, Abrams and Gill 1979: 460)

Continuing to look upon the mist-sea Wordsworth discerns in it a fracture from which issue the sounds – characteristic of much British mountain scenery – of waters running. The voice of the waters sounds 'homeless' (1805, XIII. 63; Wordsworth, Abrams and Gill 1979: 460), separated from its proper place, as it is heard only through the illusory sea of mist. It is in this sublime spectacle that 'Nature' had 'lodged/The soul, the imagination of the whole' (1805, XIII. 64–65; Wordsworth, Abrams and Gill 1979: 460):

> from the shore
> At distance not the third part of a mile
> Was a blue chasm, a fracture in the vapour,
> A deep and gloomy breathing-place, through which
> Mounted the roar of waters, torrents, streams
> Innumerable, roaring with one voice.
> The universal spectacle throughout
> Was shaped for admiration and delight,
> Grand in itself alone, but in that breach
> Through which the homeless voice of waters rose,
> That dark deep thoroughfare, had Nature lodged
> The soul, the imagination of the whole.
>
> (1805, XIII. 54–65; Wordsworth, Abrams and Gill 1979: 460)

Wordsworth goes on to describe the way in which, once the scene of the mist-sea had passed, he recognized in that scene, when the mist gave the illusion of headlands and displaced the actual sea, a 'symbol of the power of the mind to achieve dominance over the visible given' (Abrams 1971: 371). The modification of the actual becomes an image, a 'resemblance', of the constitutive capacity of 'higher minds' (1805, XIII. 87, 90; Wordsworth, Abrams and Gill 1979: 462), that creative capacity which puts those minds intimately in touch with a realm beyond sensuous reality:

> A meditation rose in me that night
> Upon the lonely mountain when the scene
> Had passed away, and it appeared to me
> The perfect image of a mighty mind,
> Of one that feeds upon infinity,

That is exalted by an under-presence,
The sense of God . . .
One function of such mind had Nature there
Exhibited by putting forth, and that
With circumstance most awful and sublime:
That domination which she oftentimes
Exerts upon the outward face of things . . .
             The Power . . .
                    which Nature thus
Thrusts forth upon the senses, is the express
Resemblance . . .
             of the glorious faculty
Which higher minds bear with them as their own . . .
They from their native selves can send abroad
Like transformation . . .
             in a world of life they live,
By sensible impressions not enthralled,
But quickened, rouzed, and made thereby more fit
To hold communion with the invisible world.
Such minds are truly from the Deity.
         (1805, XIII. 66–72, 74–78, 84–87, 89–90, 93–94, 102–106;
               Wordsworth, Abrams and Gill 1979: 460, 462, 464)

Nature thus can offer a 'resemblance' of the 'glorious faculty' of higher minds. Nature can herself intimate something beyond herself: the soul, the imagination of the whole. The 'herself' is important here. Nature is characterized as feminine ('That domination which she oftentimes/Exerts'). But the feminine is here associated with something that is not in itself of ultimate importance. Feminine nature simply directs towards the reality of ultimate importance which lies beyond nature herself. What is really of importance in this passage is the male speaker's mind, his imagination, which participates in and apprehends the ultimate mind, imagination or 'Deity'. The sublime moment is peculiarly male. Nature and the feminine can help facilitate this moment of sublime apprehension, but that is as far as it goes. Priority and ultimacy reside with the masculine while the feminine is accorded a secondary, supportive role. This metaphysics, as it were, of masculine and feminine principles pervades the entirety of *The Prelude* just as it determines Wordsworth's treatment of his sister Dorothy at the end of 'Tintern Abbey', where Dorothy is placed as a kind of silent, supplementary support to the speaker's imagination. So often in Wordsworth the feminine is associated with the sensory and the natural. As such it is valued, up to a point. Much as the 'Earth' in the 'Immortality Ode' is character-ized as feminine and is seen as having her own responsibilities and her own dignity:

> Earth fills her lap with pleasures of her own;
> Yearnings she hath in her own natural kind,
> And, even with something of a Mother's mind,
>     And no unworthy aim,
>     The homely Nurse doth all she can
> To make her Foster-child, her Inmate Man,
>     Forget the glories he hath known,
> And that imperial palace whence he came.
>
> (77–84; Gill 1984: 299)

But just as, here, the feminine Earth is seen as inferior to the spiritual glory of what is only her 'Foster-child', her inmate 'Man', so in *The Prelude* feminine nature is not of ultimate or fundamental significance. That significance is reserved for the spiritual, the invisible, the transcendental, which in contradistinction to feminine nature is associated with the masculine. Nor is it unimportant that that masculinized spiritual power is described in terms of imperial power ('that imperial palace'). In this economy the feminine is expunged by the divinely sanctioned, masculine, imperial force of spirit or imagination. No more than in the work of Edmund Burke does the feminine participate in the sublime itself.

This dominating power of masculine spirit, absorbing and transcending feminine nature's own dominating powers, goes further than just overwhelming nature. Or, rather, it overwhelms partly by appropriating and colonizing elements of the feminine. In Book XIII of *The Prelude* Wordsworth 'celebrates', as Alan Richardson has put it in an essay entitled 'Romanticism and the Colonization of the Feminine', the 'essential maternity of the fully imaginative man' (Mellor 1988: 16); or, as Gayatri Spivak has observed, Wordsworth claims for the highest mind, the full-grown male poet, 'an androgynous plenitude which would include within the self an indeterminate role of mother as well as lover' (Spivak 1981: 334):

> he whose soul hath risen
> Up to the height of feeling intellect
> Shall want no humbler tenderness, his heart
> Be tender as a nursing mother's heart;
> Of female softness shall his life be full,
> Of little loves and delicate desires,
> Mild interests and gentlest sympathies.
>
> (1805, XIII. 204–10; Wordsworth, Abrams and Gill 1979: 470)

Anne K. Mellor has summarized the typical male Romantic appropriation of the feminine as follows:

> By taking on the feminine virtues of compassion, mercy, gentle-ness and sympathy, the male Romantic poets could claim to speak with ultimate moral as well as intellectual authority. . . . By usurping the mother's womb, life-giving power, and feminine sensibilities, the male poet could claim to be God, the sole ruler of the world.
>
> Foremost among the traditionally feminine qualities colonized by this strain of masculine Romanticism is love. . . .
>
> Given the central role played by passionate love in masculine Romanticism, where love is the means by which the poet

attempts to rise on an almost Platonic ladder to the most transcendent and visionary of human experiences, and the explicit valorization of the beloved woman contained within this secular myth, we might expect a recognition of the erotic power and spiritual equality of the female to be essential to their poetry. But when we look closely at the gender implications of romantic love, we discover that rather than embracing the female as a valued other, the male lover usually effaces her into a narcissistic projection of his own self.

(Mellor 1993: 23–25)

Mellor takes the examples of Shelley and Keats to illustrate her argument:

the deceived poet in [Shelley's] *Alastor* . . . rejects the village girls and Arab maiden to seek instead his 'vision' of the ideal woman whose voice 'is like the voice of his own soul'. . . . It is the quest of the poet in [his] *Epipsychidion* who seeks . . . to become 'conscious, inseparable, one' with his beloved Emily. . . .

the consummation desired by Shelley's narrators can only be achieved through death, through the literal annihilation of the consciousness of division between the lover and his beloved. Similarly, Porphyro and Madeline [in Keats' 'The Eve of St Agnes', 1820] flee into the storm, and 'are gone'. . . .

Since the object of romantic or erotic love is not the recognition and appreciation of the beloved woman as an independent other but rather the assimilation of the female into the male (or the annihilation of any Other that threatens masculine selfhood), the woman must finally be enslaved or destroyed, must disappear or die.

(Mellor 1993: 25–26)

Feminists have argued that a comparable point can be made about the writings of William Blake. Blake may seem at times

deeply anti-sexist and anti-patriarchal, but Mary Lynn Johnson
has observed that

> antipatriarchal elements in Blake's thought are countered
> everywhere by antifeminist elements of equal or greater force.
> . . . Blake . . . allows no female character to enter the ideal
> androgynous state by absorbing a masculine element; the
> feminine side of the supposed androgyne Albion actually
> disappears when it unites with the masculine. Blake invariably
> personifies the creative genius as male, his creation as female.
> . . . As Susan Fox observes, 'No woman in any Blake poem has
> both the will and the power to initiate her own salvation, not
> even the strongest and most independent of his women,
> Oothoon'.
>
> (Gleckner and Greenberg 1989: 59)

For many of the very many female writers of the later eighteenth
and early nineteenth centuries the masculinizing of visionary
experience, of the sublime, by male writers would have presented
a problem. (For a survey of some of the women writers of the period
see Stuart Curran, 'Women readers, women writers' in Curran
1993: 177–95.) They were effectively excluded from the experience
defined by such as Wordsworth as the most important experience
in life. And the appropriation of certain key feminine characteristics by male writers would not have helped matters. Feminist
readers have seen Mary Shelley's *Frankenstein* as a satire not just on
the Romantic model of the solitary, creative imagination, but
specifically on the masculinism of that model. In 1979 Sandra
Gilbert and Susan Gubar saw the story of Frankenstein's creation
of life partly as a grotesque parody of women's biological role
(Gilbert and Gubar 1979: 213–47). Certainly, the attack on
Frankenstein's egotism in the novel can be read as an attack on male
exploitation of the female and of the feminine. Nature is identified
in the novel as female, just as in Wordsworth. Frankenstein describes
himself as having 'pursued nature to her hiding-places' (Hindle

1985: 98). In so doing, Frankenstein appropriates women's pro-creative role. As contrasted, however, with Wordsworth, the male spirit on its sublime quest is not lauded in this novel but is shown, as I suggested in chapter 3, as egotistically destructive. Mary Poovey has, furthermore, seen in the Monster created by Frankenstein an image of the monstrosity of imagining the Other in female terms. And the alienated pathos of the Monster's own narrative can be seen as analogous to the social situation of women. 'He', a male-constructed creature, tells what it is like to be born as the foil for male fantasies of power. 'In her depictions of the monster', writes Mary Poovey, 'Mary Shelley elevates feminine helplessness to the stature of myth' (Poovey 1984: 142)

Apart, however, from a work like *Frankenstein*, which may be read as directly condemning the voracious masculinism of Romantic visions of the highest self and of the sublime, many women writers of the period seem to have responded quite properly to the sublime as something from which they were, in any case, excluded; that is to say, they simply did not treat it, they actively ignored it. Margaret Homans has seen Dorothy Wordsworth – for all that Wordsworth saw her as a supportive adjunct in his poetry and for all that she acted as his supportive adjunct in real life – as effectively subverting, in her *Journals* of 1798 and 1800–1803, Wordsworth's poetic treatment of nature and of the self. Wordsworth's poetry displays his desire to celebrate the power of the observing mind over the objects it observes: nature is celebrated but what is celebrated even more is the mind's power – founded in absolute power – to see through and to transfigure the objects of perception. Natural objects are thus always being read by Wordsworth as symbolic of some higher meaning than, considered in themselves, they may be said to possess. Wordsworth may have wanted faithfully to record images of nature but his images are, as Homans puts it, always 'killed into meaning'; 'Wordsworth's aim is not the preservation of images in itself, although this is important, but the pursuit of infinitude and eternity' (Homans 1986: 51–52).

Homans reads Dorothy's refusal, in her *Journals*, to find infinite and eternal meaning in the images she draws of nature as a subversion of her brother's overweening male attempt to impose meaning on experience. Her *Journals* record nature in a way that genuinely allows nature a life of its own:

> This discourse that is resistant to symbol making is apparent almost everywhere in the Alfoxden and Grasmere journals of 1798–1803. Instead of the relation of symbolism, which suggests a hierarchical ordering of two terms, she presents nature gratuitously working in tandem with the human mind. Since she guarantees that she never imposes meaning on nature, we trust that details that appear to be symbolic of events in the writer's life are actually just the register of nature's free paralleling of human life. To say that she erases entirely the traces of her own creative act would be to suggest incorrectly that her mode is merely covert symbolism; she makes us doubt that there ever was a creative act. No rhetorical term fully conveys the insubordination of these free parallels between human and natural, in which there is no order of hierarchy. Her parallels have meaning only if nature has as full a value as the human experience, and it can have that full value only if it is not portrayed as subordinate to the human.

> (Homans 1986: 54)

Dorothy's allowance of the autonomy of natural life is apparent in an entry she made in her Grasmere Journal for 31 October 1802, where the human perceiver seems simply co-existent with the scene perceived:

> I walked to the top of the hill and looked at Rydale. I was much affected when I stood upon the second bar of Sara's Gate. The lake was perfectly still, the sun shone on hill and vale, the distant birch trees looked like large golden Flowers. Nothing else in colour was distinct and separate, but all the beautiful

colours seemed to be melted into one another, and joined together in one mass, so that there were no differences, though an endless variety, when one tried to find it out.

(Darbishire 1958: 209)

Homans sees a subtle female project at work in Dorothy Wordsworth's insistence in her *Journals* on finding true images of nature. In the process, her passivity in the face of her brother's obsession with the imperial self asserts itself as an alternative mode of defining subjectivity and value:

what is important is not just Dorothy Wordsworth's own project to retain for nature the status of an equal, both in her rhetoric and as a theme, but most especially her practicing this project as a part of reading and literalizing or enacting her brother's words. While she would write this way in any case, she also puts her texts at the service of his compelling demand, letting his texts appropriate hers for the completion of their own design. . . . And yet, because she enacts his words so much more faithfully than he does himself, she covertly transforms this passive female duty back into her own project, which is, implicitly and intermittently, critical of William's apocalyptic tendencies. Showing him that meaning can take place when both signifier and referent are present, she speaks for the literal nature that is most often silent within his texts.

(Homans 1986: 56)

'[W]omen writers' of the end of the eighteenth and beginning of the nineteenth centuries 'often turned away', writes Meena Alexander, 'from the abstractions or high sublimity of their male counterparts, to the concrete acts of nurture and care associated with maternity' (Alexander 1989: 68). The literalness and concreteness of Dorothy Wordsworth's interest in nature leads Alexander to make a point concerning Dorothy's writing which is comparable to that made by Margaret Homans. For both commentators there is something which runs distinctively counter to William Wordsworth's masculinized and egocentric sublime in Dorothy Wordsworth's rejection of the sublime:

> The visible world . . . in Dorothy's finest writings. . . . gathers powers and luminosity precisely to the extent to which it is shorn of the overt hold of the self. For her the literal is distanced from the turbulence of imaginative need and turns mystical in its lack, in the subtraction from it of the mind's hold. And so for Dorothy Wordsworth, in contrast to her brother William, the image of a building or shelter, a trope for the self, comes often to stand for an actual dwelling, not a textual one, a shelter that is shared with a loved other. Gender would seem crucial, the woman's sense of self intrinsically bound up with the lives of others, rather than developed in exclusion from them. A striking correlative to such a sense of self is that the powerful counter-world of symbolism is then cast aside in favour of the actual.
>
> (Alexander 1989: 88)

This idea that women's writing – suspicious of the masculinized and egocentric sublime – commits itself more characteristically to an ideal of actual, shared human experience is one that Alexander also explores in writings by Mary Wollstonecraft and Mary Shelley. Another commentator interested in developing a way of reading women's writing, specifically the poetry of the period, is Isobel Armstrong. As she says in a paper entitled 'The Gush of the Feminine: how can we read women's poetry of the Romantic Period?' (Armstrong 1995), we have had two hundred years to evolve ways of reading male poets. To read the newly re-emergent women poets '[a]nother politics, another epistemology, another theory of language, are required' (Armstrong 1995). Armstrong takes as a test case Anna Laetitia Barbauld's poem 'Inscription for an Ice-House':

Stranger, approach! within this iron door
Thrice locked and bolted, this rude arch beneath
That vaults with ponderous stone the cell; confined
By man, the great magician, who controuls
Fire, earth and air, and genii of the storm,
And bends the most remote and opposite things
To do him service and perform his will, –
A giant sits; stern Winter; here he piles,
While summer glows around, and southern gales
Dissolve the fainting world, his treasured snows
Within the rugged cave. – Stranger, approach!
He will not cramp thy limbs with sudden age,
Nor wither with his touch the coyest flower
That decks thy scented hair. Indignant here,
Like fettered Sampson when his might was spent
In puny feats to glad the festive halls
Of Gaza's wealthy sons; or he who sat
Midst laughing girls submiss, and patient twirled
The slender spindle in his sinewy grasp;
The rugged power, fair Pleasure's minister,
Exerts his art to deck the genial board;
Congeals the melting peach, the nectarine smooth,
Burnished and glowing from the sunny wall:
Darts sudden frost into the crimson veins
Of the moist berry; moulds the sugared hail:
Cools with his icy breath our flowing cups;
Or gives to the fresh dairy's nectared bowls
A quicker zest. Sullen he plies his task,
And on his shaking fingers counts the weeks
Of lingering Summer, mindful of his hour
To rush in whirlwinds forth, and rule the year.

(Barbauld 1825: I. 188–89)

Armstrong invokes Edmund Burke on the sublime and on
the beautiful as she discovers a gendered debate at play in the
poem:

> Winter was traditionally the quintessentially sublime season.
> . . . In Mrs Barbauld's poem, however, Winter is associated not
> with transcendence and self-overcoming but with technology
> and instrumental control. In an apparent reversal of the master/
> slave power relationship, Winter is 'fair Pleasure's minister'.
> Burke had said explicitly that the sublime is superior to pleasure
> and transcends utility. In 'Inscription for an Ice-House', sublime
> Winter is subordinated to both. The erotic, feminized and
> 'beautiful' Burkean epithets, 'melting' and 'smooth', used in the
> poem to describe the preserved fruits, collaborate against
> him. His violence is neutralized, like 'fettered Sampson', or like
> Hercules, who was condemned to dress in women's clothes
> and spin amongst women. The comedy of a sublime expending
> itself in demasculinized 'puny feats' or forced virtually to change
> gender, cross dressing in the women's domain as gross
> 'sinewy' power clumsily handles the small, beautiful object, the
> 'slender' spindle, makes free use of sexual innuendo. Winter
> does not understand women's arts, culture, or sexuality.
>
> (Armstrong 1995)

But 'Inscription for an Ice-House' does not, as Armstrong points
out, merely affirm the beautiful in opposition to the sublime.
There is a conflict going on in the poem not only between 'man'
and 'Winter' ('man . . . / . . . bends the most remote and opposite
things/To do him service') but also between the feminine and
Winter:

> Delilah gains power through seduction: the 'laughing girls' . . .
> gain power through ridicule. Sinisterly, the syntax slides, just as
> in the master/slave relationship of man and nature. 'Midst
> laughing girls *submiss*' (my emphasis) makes it possible for

Winter-Hercules to be 'submiss' to the laughing girls and the laughing girls to be 'submiss' to Hercules. That is to say, the *structure* of relationships has not really changed with the advent of the technology which can control the climate of the icehouse, despite the seeming reversal of power. Women, locked in the icehouse with Winter, live unequally with him, forced into ruses to control him. The delicate flowers in the scented hair of the apostrophised visitor mark her vulnerability.

(Armstrong 1995)

'What makes women so vulnerable', asks Armstrong, 'so little able simply to reverse the place and power of sublime Winter?' (Armstrong 1995). The answer, she says, is women's fertility, their reproductive power, their sexuality. The poem is crammed with images associated with this sensuous power: the 'moist berry', the 'flowing cups' and 'nectared bowls'. This power is subject to Winter's power but at the same time oddly escapes it. 'The category of the beautiful cannot contain this generative excess', notes Armstrong, 'but excess seems to be women's greatest problem as well as her greatest triumph' (Armstrong 1995). Armstrong turns to Thomas Robert Malthus' (1766–1834) *An Essay on the Principle of Population* (1798) in order to explain the problem. Malthus argued that human population would soon exceed the means of subsistence. And it was the fertility and child-bearing productivity of women that stood at the root of the matter: 'Nature, he says, is a Cleopatra (another seducer), squandering production in overpopulation which results in shortage' (Armstrong 1995). In Barbauld's poem it looks at first as if Malthus is being refuted. The wealthy household can use its icehouse to preserve nature's productions: Winter, the power associated with shortage, can be made to help sustain life. The difficulty as far as the feminine is concerned is that sustenance is gained actually at the expense of female fertility, which is in a state of suspended animation, frozen, its life denied ('Darts sudden frost into the crimson veins').

'Feminine fertility', says Armstrong, 'is constrained and uneasy, profoundly doubtful about an artificial and death-bringing preservation of its being. The Malthusian fix is not that easy to evade' (Armstrong 1995).

Armstrong finds a further illustration of the difficult place of the feminine in this poem, when she writes:

> Whereas 'man' controls resources and participates in the exchange of 'remote and opposite things' . . . women are confined to a narrower range of tasks and objects. Domestic experience in this poem is broken down into a series of discrete items and, through a quasi-metonymic use of the definite article, is constructed as a continual repetition of the same structure – 'the' spindle, board, peach, nectarine, wall, berry, hail, dairy. The division of labour, one remembers, takes place as a series of infinite repetitions of the same discrete task. . . . The semantic relation of parts and parturition hovers in the language of the text. It is as if a grammar of parts has been made the foundation of women's knowledge and experience – a feminine cogito recognised as fragmenting even when it carries the empowerment of giving birth. Winter, serving his time in the domestic world, can escape to ravage the earth. The women belonging to the world of the icehouse do not escape from him. This is the reverse of the Persephone myth. The Persephone figure is misled: she will indeed be afflicted with 'cramp' as the 'crimson veins' are seized up from within with frost, a sinister figure for the frozen blockage which prevents movement and circulation in a universe of parts. Instead she participates in the ultimate metonymic substitution of parts, of tomb for womb.
>
> (Armstrong 1995)

Finding a sexual politics at the heart of this poem, Isobel Armstrong is helping to produce a strategy for reading a literary work which does not fulfil notions of meaning based on the productions of male writers but which is, nevertheless, carrying a comparable weight of meaning. It is just that the meaning is different from what has come to be accepted as the meaning of (predominantly male) writers of the late eighteenth and early nineteenth centuries.

The period of the late eighteenth and early nineteenth centuries witnessed the emergence of many Western cultural tensions which, however remote the period may sometimes seem, are still being worked out in the late twentieth century. The conflict between political radicalism and political reaction, the conflict between the claims of the individual and the claims of community, the conflict between the interests of feeling or imagination and the interests of reason and sceptical inquiry, the conflict between spiritual sympathy and materialist conviction, all receive recognizably modern formulations in the period. In a just comment M.H. Abrams spoke of the period in terms of 'the cataclysmic coming into being of the world to which we are by now becoming fairly accustomed' (Frye 1963: 30). So it is not surprising that the literature of the period has been ceaselessly reinterpreted and reconstructed by later commentators who have themselves only been ringing the changes on paradigms laid down in the period itself. Issues concerning the representation of gender, which were at the heart of the period itself, have fairly recently begun to occupy centre stage in considerations of the literature of the period. And the development of a hermeneutics for reading the literary productions of women writers is one of the principal directions that criticism of the Romantic period will now take.

# PRIMARY SOURCES

Some of the primary sources referred to in the text of this book are listed in the Bibliography under editors' rather than authors' names. The following is a list of these sources under authors' names.

Blake, William (1970) *The Poetry and Prose of William Blake*, edited by David V. Erdman and Harold Bloom, 1st published 1965, reprinted with revision, New York, Doubleday and Co.

Burns, Robert (1968) *The Poems and Songs of Robert Burns*, 3 vols, edited by James Kinsley, Oxford, Oxford University Press.

Byron, Lord (1970) *Poetical Works*, edited by Frederick Page, 1st published 1904, 3rd edn [corrected by John Jump] London, Oxford and New York, Oxford University Press.

Clare, John (1984) *The Later Poems of John Clare. 1837–1864*, 2 vols, edited by Eric Robinson and David Powell, Oxford, Clarendon Press.

Coleridge, Samuel Taylor (1907) *'Biographia Literaria'. By S.T. Coleridge*, 2 vols, edited by J. Shawcross, Oxford, Clarendon Press.

—— (1912) *The Complete Poetical Works of Samuel Taylor Coleridge*, 2 vols, edited by Ernest Hartley Coleridge, Oxford, Clarendon Press.

—— (1972) *Samuel Taylor Coleridge. Lay Sermons*, edited by R.J. White, part 6 of *The Collected Works of Samuel Taylor Coleridge*, General Editor: Kathleen Coburn, Princeton, NJ, Princeton University Press.

—— (1972) *Samuel Taylor Coleridge. On the Constitution of the Church and State According to the Idea of Each*, edited by John Barrell, London, J.M. Dent and Sons.

—— (1987) *Samuel Taylor Coleridge. Lectures 1808–1819 On Literature*, 2 vols, edited by R.A. Foakes, part 5 of *The Collected Works of Samuel Taylor Coleridge*, General Editor: Kathleen Coburn, London, Routledge and Kegan Paul and Princeton, NJ, Princeton University Press.

Cowper, William (1931) *Poems by William Cowper*, edited by Hugh l'Anson Fausset, Everyman's Library, London, J.M. Dent and Sons.

Crabbe, George (1988) *The Complete Poetical Works*, 3 vols, edited by Norma Dalrymple-Champneys and Arthur Pollard, Oxford, Clarendon Press.

Gray, Thomas (1969) *The Poems of Thomas Gray, William Collins and Oliver Goldsmith*, edited by Roger Lonsdale, Longman Annotated English Poets, London, Longman.

Hazlitt, William (1930–34) *The Complete Works of William Hazlitt*, 21 vols, edited by P.P. Howe, London and Toronto, J.M. Dent.

Hogg, James (1970) *Selected Poems*, edited by Douglas S. Mack, Oxford, Clarendon Press.

Kant, Immanuel (1970) *Kant's Political Writings*, edited by Hans Reiss, translated by H.B. Nisbet, Cambridge, Cambridge University Press.

Keats, John (1952) *The Letters of John Keats*, edited by Maurice Buxton Forman, 1st published 1931, 4th edition London, New York and Toronto, Oxford University Press.

Keats, John (1970) *The Poems of John Keats*, edited by Miriam Allott, Longman Annotated English Poets, London, Longman.

Landor, Walter Savage (1937) *The Poetical Works of Walter Savage Landor*, 3 vols, edited by Stephen Wheeler, Oxford, Clarendon Press.

Marx, Karl (1983) *The Portable Karl Marx*, edited by Eugene Kamenka, Harmondsworth, Penguin Books.

Peacock, Thomas Love, (1924–34) *The Works of Thomas Love Peacock*, 10 vols, edited by H.F.B. Brett-Smith and C.E. Jones, *The Halliford Edition*, London, Constable and New York, Gabriel Wells.

—— (1948) *The Novels of Thomas Love Peacock*, edited by David Garnett, London, Rupert Hart-Davis.

Pope, Alexander (1961) *Alexander Pope. Pastoral Poetry and An Essay on Criticism*, edited by E. Audra and Aubrey Williams, *The Twickenham Edition of the Poems of Alexander Pope*, vol. 1, General Editor: John Butt, London, Methuen.

Shelley, Mary (1947) *Mary Shelley's Journal*, edited by Frederick L. Jones, Norman, OK, University of Oklahoma Press.

—— (1985) *Frankenstein or, The Modern Prometheus*, edited by Maurice Hindle, 1st published 1818, Harmondsworth, Penguin Books.

Shelley, Percy Bysshe (1965) *The Complete Works of Percy Bysshe Shelley*, 10 vols, edited by Roger Ingpen and Walter E. Peck, London, Ernest Benn and New York, Gordan Press.

—— (1968) *Shelley. Poetical Works*, edited by Thomas Hutchinson, 1st published 1905, London, Oxford University Press.

Smith, Charlotte (1993) *The Poems of Charlotte Smith*, edited by Stuart Curran, New York and Oxford, Oxford University Press.

Southey, Robert (1909) *Poems of Robert Southey*, edited by Maurice H. Fitzgerald, London, Oxford University Press.

Tennyson, Alfred (1991) *Alfred Lord Tennyson. Selected Poems*, edited by Aidan Day, London, Penguin Books.

Thomson, James (1981) *'The Seasons'*, edited by James Sambrook, Oxford, Clarendon Press.

Wordsworth, Dorothy (1958) *Journals of Dorothy Wordsworth*, edited by Helen Darbishire, London, New York and Toronto, Oxford University Press.

Wordsworth, William (1972) *The Poetical Works of William Wordsworth*, vol. 5, *The Excursion, The Recluse*, edited by Ernest de Selincourt and Helen Darbishire, 1st published 1949, Oxford, Clarendon Press.

—— (1974) *The Prose Works of William Wordsworth*, 3 vols, edited by

W.J.B. Owen and Jane Worthington Smyser, Oxford, Oxford University Press.

—— (1975) *The Salisbury Plain Poems of William Wordsworth*, edited by Stephen Gill, Ithaca, NY, Cornell University Press and Hassocks, Sussex, Harvester Press.

—— (1976) *Wordsworth and Coleridge: 'Lyrical Ballads'*, edited by R.L. Brett and A.R. Jones, 1st published 1963, London, Methuen.

—— (1979) *'The Prelude' 1799, 1805, 1850*, edited by Jonathan Wordsworth, M.H. Abrams and Stephen Gill, New York and London, W.W. Norton and Co.

—— (1984) *William Wordsworth*, edited by Stephen Gill, The Oxford Authors, Oxford and New York, Oxford University Press.

# BIBLIOGRAPHY

Abrams, M.H. (1953) *The Mirror and the Lamp: Romantic Theory and the Critical Tradition*, New York, Oxford University Press.

—— (1971) *Natural Supernaturalism. Tradition and Revolution in Romantic Literature*, New York, W.W. Norton and Co.

—— (1993) *A Glossary of Literary Terms*, 6th edition, Fort Worth, Harcourt Brace Jovanovich College Publishers.

Akenside, Mark (1772) *The Poems of Mark Akenside, M.D.*, London, printed by W. Bowyer and J. Nichols.

Alexander, Meena (1989) *Women in Romanticism*, Basingstoke and London, Macmillan Education.

Allott, Miriam (ed) (1970) *The Poems of John Keats*, Longman Annotated English Poets, London, Longman.

Armstrong, Isobel (1995) 'The Gush of the Feminine: How Can We Read Women's Poetry of the Romantic Period?' in Paula R. Feldman and Theresa M. Kelley (eds) *Romantic Women Writers: Voices and Countervoices*, Hanover and London, University Press of New England.

Audra, E. and Williams, Aubrey (eds) (1961) *Alexander Pope. Pastoral Poetry and An Essay on Criticism, The Twickenham Edition of the Poems of Alexander Pope*, General Editor: John Butt, vol. 1, London, Methuen.

Austen, Jane [1814] (1980) *Mansfield Park*, edited by Tony Tanner, 1st published 1966, London, Penguin Books.

Babbit, Irving (1919) *Rousseau and Romanticism*, Boston and New York, Riverside Press.

Barbauld, Anna Laetitia (1825) *The Works of Anna Laetitia Barbauld. With a Memoir by Lucy Aiken*, 2 vols, London, printed for Longman, Hurst, Rees, Orme, Brown and Green.

Barrell, John (ed) (1972) *Samuel Taylor Coleridge. On the Constitution of the Church and State According to the Idea of Each*, London, J.M. Dent and Sons.

Barzun, Jacques (1944) *Romanticism and the Modern Ego*, 1st published 1943, republished 1944, London, Secker and Warburg.

—— (1962) *Classic, Romantic and Modern*, 1st published 1961, republished 1962, London, Secker and Warburg.

Beattie, James (1831) *The Poetical Works of James Beattie*, The Aldine Edition of the British Poets, London, William Pickering.

Belsey, Catherine (1986) 'The Romantic Construction of the Unconscious', in Francis Barker, Peter Hulme, Margaret Iveson, Diana Loxley (eds) *Literature, Politics and Theory, Papers from the Essex Conference 1976-84*, London and New York, Methuen.

Bloom, Harold (ed) (1970) *Romanticism and Consciousness. Essays in Criticism*, New York, W.W. Norton and Co.

—— and Trilling, Lionel (eds) (1973) *Romantic Poetry and Prose*, The Oxford Anthology of English Literature, New York, London and Toronto, Oxford University Press.

Bowra, C.M. (1950) *The Romantic Imagination*, London, Oxford University Press.

Brett, R.L. and Jones, A.R. (eds) (1976) *Wordsworth and Coleridge. 'Lyrical Ballads'* 1st published 1963, London, Methuen, [1798 edition with the additional 1800 poems and the Preface].

Brett-Smith, H.F.B. and Jones, C.E. (eds) (1924–34) *The Works of Thomas Love Peacock*, 10 vols, *The Halliford Edition*, London, Constable and New York, Gabriel Wells.

Burke, Edmund [1790] (1986) *Reflections on the Revolution in France*, edited by Conor Cruise O'Brien, London, Penguin Books.

—— [1757] (1990) *A Philosophical Enquiry into the Origins of our Ideas of the Sublime and Beautiful*, edited by Adam Phillips, World's Classics, Oxford and New York, Oxford University Press.

Butler, Marilyn (1981) *Romantics, Rebels and Reactionaries. English Literature and its Background 1760-1830*, Oxford, Oxford University Press.

Calder, Angus (1987) *Byron*, Milton Keynes and Philadelphia, Open University Press.

Campbell, Thomas (1799) *The Pleasures of Hope . . . With Other Poems*, Edinburgh, printed for Mundell and Son.

Coleridge, Ernest Hartley (ed) (1912) *The Complete Poetical Works of Samuel Taylor Coleridge*, 2 vols, Oxford, Clarendon Press.

Colvin, Sidney (1881) *Landor*, English Men of Letters, London, Macmillan and Co.

Copley, Stephen and Whale, John (eds) (1992) *Beyond Romanticism: New Approaches to Texts and Contexts 1780-1832*, London and New York, Routledge.

Courthope, W.J. (1885) *The Liberal Movement in English Literature*, London, John Murray.

Curran, Stuart (ed) (1993) *The Cambridge Companion to British Romanticism*, Cambridge, Cambridge University Press.

—— (ed) (1993a) *The Poems of Charlotte Smith*, New York and Oxford, Oxford University Press.

Dalrymple-Champneys, Norma and Pollard, Arthur (eds) (1988) *George Crabbe. The Complete Poetical Works*, 3 vols, Oxford, Clarendon Press.

Darbishire, Helen (ed) (1958) *Journals of Dorothy Wordsworth*, London, New York and Toronto, Oxford University Press.

Day, Aidan (ed) (1991) *Alfred Lord Tennyson. Selected Poems*, London, Penguin Books.

de Man, Paul (1983) *Blindness and Insight. Essays in the Rhetoric of Contemporary Criticism*, 2nd edition, London, Methuen.

de Selincourt, Ernest and Darbishire, Helen (eds) (1972) *The Poetical Works of William Wordsworth*, vol. 5, *The Excursion, The Recluse*, 1st published 1949, Oxford, Clarendon Press.

Dowden, Edward (1897) *The French Revolution and English Literature*, London, Kegan Paul.

Drabble, Margaret (ed) (1985) *The Oxford Companion to English Literature*, 5th edition, Oxford, Oxford University Press.

Edgeworth, Maria [1795] (1805) *Letters for Literary Ladies*, 3rd edition, Harlow, printed for J. Johnson.

Eichner, Hans (ed) (1972) *'Romantic' and its Cognates. The European History of a Word*, Manchester, Manchester University Press.

*Encyclopaedia Britannica* (1910–11), 11th edition, 29 vols, New York, The Encyclopaedia Britannica Company.

Erdman, David V. (1954) *Blake: Prophet Against Empire. A Poet's Interpretation of the History of his own Times*, Princeton, Princeton University Press.

Erdman, David V. and Bloom, Harold (eds) (1970) *The Poetry and Prose of William Blake*, 1st published 1965, reprinted with revision, New York, Doubleday and Co.

Fitzgerald, Maurice H. (ed) (1909) *Poems of Robert Southey*, London, Oxford University Press.

Foakes, R.A. (ed) (1987) *Samuel Taylor Coleridge. Lectures 1808-1819 On Literature*, 2 vols, part 5 of *The Collected Works of Samuel Taylor Coleridge*, General Editor: Kathleen Coburn, London, Routledge and Kegan Paul and Princeton, NJ, Princeton University Press.

Forman, Maurice Buxton (ed) (1952) *The Letters of John Keats*,
1st published 1931, 4th edition, London, New York and
Toronto, Oxford University Press.

Frye, Northrop (1962) *Fearful Symmetry. A Study of William Blake*, 1st
published 1947, Boston, Beacon.

—— (ed) (1963) *Romanticism Reconsidered*, New York and London,
Columbia University Press.

Garnett, David (ed) (1948) *The Novels of Thomas Love Peacock*, London,
Rupert Hart-Davis.

Gay, Peter (1973) *The Enlightenment: An Interpretation*, in 2 vols: *The Rise
of Modern Paganism* and *The Science of Freedom*, 1st published in
Great Britain 1970, London, Weidenfeld and Nicolson; republished
1973, London, Wildwood House.

Gilbert, Sandra and Gubar, Susan (1979) *The Madwoman in the Attic: The
Woman Writer and the Nineteenth Century Literary Imagination*, New
Haven, Yale University Press.

Gill, Stephen (ed) (1975) *The Salisbury Plain Poems of William Wordsworth*,
Ithaca, NY, Cornell University Press and Hassocks, Sussex,
Harvester Press.

—— (ed) (1984) *William Wordsworth*, The Oxford Authors, Oxford and
New York, Oxford University Press.

—— (1989) *William Wordsworth. A Life*, Oxford, Clarendon Press.

Gleckner, Robert F. and Greenberg, Mark L. (eds) (1989) *Approaches to
Teaching Blake's Songs of Innocence and of Experience*, New York,
Modern Language Association of America.

Godwin, William [1793] (1985) *Enquiry Concerning Political Justice and its
Influence on Morals and Happiness*, edited by Isaac Kramnick,
London, Penguin Books.

Guerard, Albert (1942) *The France of Tomorrow*, Cambridge, MA, Harvard
University Press.

Hamilton, Paul (1983) *Coleridge's Poetics*, Oxford, Blackwell.

Hanley, Keith (ed) (1981) *Walter Savage Landor. Selected Poetry and Prose*, Manchester, Carcanet Press.

Hartman, Geoffrey (1977) *Wordsworth's Poetry 1787-1814*, 1st published 1964, New Haven and London, Yale University Press.

Hindle, Maurice (ed) (1985) *Mary Shelley. Frankenstein or, The Modern Prometheus*, 1st published 1818; Harmondsworth, Penguin Books.

Holmes, Richard (1976) *Shelley. The Pursuit*, 1st published 1974, London, Quartet Books.

Homans, Margaret (1986) *Bearing the Word. Language and Female Experience in Nineteenth Century Women's Writing*, Chicago, IL and London, University of Chicago Press.

Howe, P.P. (ed) (1930–34) *The Complete Works of William Hazlitt*, 21 vols, London and Toronto, J.M. Dent.

Hurd, Richard (1762) *Letters on Chivalry and Romance*, 2nd edition, London, printed for A. Millar *et al.*

Hutchinson, Thomas (ed) (1968) *Shelley. Poetical Works*, 1st published 1905, London, Oxford University Press.

I'Anson Fausset, Hugh (ed) (1931) *Poems by William Cowper*, Everyman's Library, London, J.M. Dent and Sons.

Ingpen, Roger and Peck, Walter E. (eds) (1965) *The Complete Works of Percy Bysshe Shelley*, 10 vols, London, Ernest Benn and New York, Gordan Press.

Jacobus, Mary (1976) *Tradition and Experiment in Wordsworth's 'Lyrical Ballads' (1798)*, Oxford, Clarendon Press.

Jones, Edmund D. (ed) (1922) *English Critical Essays (Sixteenth, Seventeenth and Eighteenth Centuries)*, The World's Classics, London, New York and Toronto, Oxford University Press.

Jones, Frederick L. (ed) (1947) *Mary Shelley's Journal*, Norman, OK, University of Oklahoma Press.

Kamenka, Eugene (ed) (1983) *The Portable Karl Marx*, Harmondsworth, Penguin Books.

Kinsley, James (ed) (1968) *The Poems and Songs of Robert Burns*, 3 vols, Oxford, Oxford University Press.

Leighton, Angela (1984) *Shelley and the Sublime. An Interpretation of the Major Poems*, Cambridge, Cambridge University Press.

Levinson, Marjorie (1986) *Wordsworth's Great Period Poems. Four Essays*, Cambridge, Cambridge University Press.

Lonsdale, Roger (ed) (1969) *The Poems of Thomas Gray, William Collins and Oliver Goldsmith*, Longman Annotated Poets, London, Longman.

—— (ed) (1990) *Eighteenth Century Women Poets. An Oxford Anthology*, 1st published 1989; paperback edition 1990, Oxford, Oxford University Press.

Lovejoy, Arthur O. (1924) 'On the Discrimination of Romanticisms', *Publications of the Modern Language Association of America*, 39, 1924, pp.229–53.

McGann, Jerome (1983) *The Romantic Ideology. A Critical Investigation*, Chicago, IL and London, University of Chicago Press.

—— (ed) (1994) *The New Oxford Book of Romantic Period Verse*, Oxford and New York, Oxford University Press.

Mack, Douglas S. (ed) (1970) *James Hogg. Selected Poems*, Oxford, Clarendon Press.

Madden, Lionel (ed) (1972) *Robert Southey. The Critical Heritage*, London and Boston, Routledge and Kegan Paul.

Mayo, Robert (1954) 'The Contemporaneity of the *Lyrical Ballads*',

*Publications of the Modern Language Association of America*, 69, 1954, pp.486-522.

Mellor, Anne K. (ed) (1988) *Romanticism and Feminism*, Bloomington, IN and Indianapolis, Indiana University Press.

—— (1993) *Romanticism and Gender*, New York and London, Routledge.

Moorman, Mary (1968) *William Wordsworth. A Biography. The Early Years 1770–1803*, 1st published 1957, London, Oxford and New York, Oxford University Press.

—— (ed) (1971) *The Journals of Dorothy Wordsworth: The Alfoxden Journal (1798), The Grasmere Journals (1800–3)*, Oxford, Oxford University Press.

Nichol Smith, David (ed) (1926) *The Oxford Book of Eighteenth Century Verse*, Oxford, Clarendon Press.

Owen, W.J.B. and Smyser, Jane Worthington (eds) (1974) *The Prose Works of William Wordsworth*, 3 vols, Oxford, Oxford University Press.

Page, Frederick (ed) (1970) *Byron. Poetical Works*, 1st published 1904, 3rd edition [corrected by John Jump] London, Oxford and New York, Oxford University Press.

Paine, Thomas [1791, 1792] (1985) *Rights of Man*, introd. by Eric Foner, London, Penguin Books.

Poovey, Mary (1984) *The Proper Lady and the Woman Writer. Ideology as Style in the Works of Mary Wollstonecraft, Mary Shelley, and Jane Austen*, Chicago, IL and London, University of Chicago Press.

Porter, Roy and Teich, Mikuláš (eds) (1988) *Romanticism in National Context*, Cambridge, Cambridge University Press.

Prickett, Stephen (1989) *England and the French Revolution*, London, Macmillan Education.

Reed, Arden (ed) (1984) *Romanticism and Language*, London, Methuen.

Reiss, Hans (ed) (1970) *Kant's Political Writings*, translated by H.B. Nisbet, Cambridge, Cambridge University Press.

Robinson, Eric and Powell, David (eds) (1984) *The Later Poems of John Clare. 1837-1864*, 2 vols, Oxford, Clarendon Press.

Roe, Nicholas (1988) *Wordsworth and Coleridge. The Radical Years*, Oxford, Oxford University Press.

Roper, Derek (ed) (1987) *Wordsworth and Coleridge: 'Lyrical Ballads' 1805*, 3rd edition, Plymouth, Northcote House.

Rousseau, Jean-Jacques [1762] (1968) *The Social Contract*, translated by Maurice Cranston, London, Penguin Books.

—— [1782] (1979) *Reveries of the Solitary Walker*, translated by Peter France, London, Penguin Books.

Sambrook, James (ed) (1981) *James Thomson. 'The Seasons'*, Oxford, Clarendon Press.

Scott, Walter [1814] (1986) *Waverley; or, 'Tis Sixty Years Since*, edited by Claire Lamont, World's Classics, Oxford, Oxford University Press.

Shadwell, Thomas (1670) *The Sullen Lovers: or, The Impertinents. A Comedy*, London, printed for Henry Herringman.

Shaw, Thomas B. (1864), *A History of English Literature, New Edition, Enlarged and Re-Written by William Smith*, 1st published 1846, St Petersburg, London, John Murray.

Shawcross, J. (ed) (1907) *'Biographia Literaria'. By S.T. Coleridge*, 2 vols, Oxford, Clarendon Press.

Simpson, David (1987) *Wordsworth's Historical Imagination. The Poetry of Displacement*, New York and London, Methuen.

Smith, Charlotte [1793] (1987) *The Old Manor House*, introd. by Janet Todd, London and New York, Pandora Press.

Smith, Logan Pearsall (1925) *Words and Idioms. Studies in the English Language*, London, Constable and Co.

Southey, Robert (1823) *The Minor Poems of Robert Southey*, 3 vols, London, printed for Longman, Hurst, Rees, Orme and Brown.

Spivak, Gayatri Chakravorty (1981) 'Sex and History in *The Prelude* (1805): Books Nine to Thirteen', *Texas Studies in Literature and Language*, vol. 23, 1981, pp.324–60.

Stevenson, W.H. and Erdman, David V. (eds) (1971) *The Poems of William Blake*, London, Longman.

Thompson, E.P. (1991) *The Making of the English Working Class*, 1st published 1963, reprinted 1991, London, Penguin Books.

Tieghem, Paul van (1930) *Le Preromantisme. Etudes d'Historie Littéraire Européenne*, II, Paris, Librairie Felix Alcan.

Warton, Joseph (1756) *An Essay on the Writings and Genius of Pope*, vol. 1, London.

—— (1822) *The Poems of T. Warton and J. Warton*, The British Poets, vol. 68, Chiswick, printed by C. Whittingham.

Warton, Thomas (1774-81) *The History of English Poetry from the Close of the Eleventh Century to the Commencement of the Eighteenth Century*, 3 vols, London, printed for J. Dodsley *et al.*

Wellek, René (1949) 'The Concept of "Romanticism" in Literary History: I. The Term "Romantic" and Its Derivatives', *Comparative Literature*, vol. 1, no. 1 (Winter 1949), pp. 1–23; 'II. The Unity of European Romanticism', *Comparative Literature*, vol. 1, no. 2 (Spring 1949), pp. 147–72.

Wheeler, Stephen (ed) (1937) *The Poetical Works of Walter Savage Landor*, 3 vols, Oxford, Clarendon Press.

White, R.J. (ed) (1972) *Samuel Taylor Coleridge. Lay Sermons*, part 6 of *The Collected Works of Samuel Taylor Coleridge*, General Editor: Kathleen Coburn, Princeton, NJ, Princeton University Press.

Williams, Helen Maria (1792) *Letters Written in France in the Summer 1790, To a Friend in England*, 3rd edition, London, printed for T. Cadell.

Wollstonecraft, Mary [1792] (1992) *A Vindication of the Rights of Woman*, introd. by Miriam Brody, 1st published 1975, London, Penguin Books.

Woodring, Carl (1970) *Politics in English Romantic Poetry*, Cambridge, MA, Harvard University Press.

Wordsworth, Jonathan, Abrams, M.H. and Gill, Stephen (eds) (1979) *William Wordsworth. 'The Prelude' 1799, 1805, 1850*, New York and London, W.W. Norton and Co.

Wu, Duncan (ed) (1994) *Romanticism. An Anthology*, Oxford and Cambridge, MA, Blackwell.